SUNDARI

SUNDARI

BY ROCKY DAVIS

A BARRE/WESTOVER BOOK

Barre Publishing, Barre, Massachusetts

DISTRIBUTED BY CROWN PUBLISHERS, INC., NEW YORK

© 1974 by Jane L. Davis
First publication December, 1974

Library of Congress Catalog Card Number: 74-22552

Printed in the United States of America

Published simultaneously in Canada by General Publishing Company Limited

Designed by Shari de Miskey

Acknowledgments

So many people have helped to make this book a reality that it would be impossible to name them all or thank them individually. Nevertheless I hope that those whose names do not appear on this page will know they have my appreciation. Some, longer suffering than others, deserve honorable mention. First among them is my husband, Bob, who now has a small fortune invested in waste paper. His tolerance and forbearance are infinite. My children, Rob, Rod, Kristy, and Jan, have my gratitude for helping to make Sundari what she is, for accepting her and loving her.

Without Charlotte Bush, who spent long hours and reams of film photographing Sundari, this book would never have been begun. It was she who insisted that Sundari's story had to be told and proceeded on the assumption that I could do it.

My affectionate thanks go to Chris Herklotz, who learned to love our leopard, deciphered my handwriting, and did much of the initial typing before she had to leave India.

And, finally, my deep appreciation and sincere thanks go to Bart McDowell for his time, effort, and patience with a novice in her first foray into literary endeavor. Without his encouragement this book would never have been finished.

For Bob
who didn't think I would

1

AS I write, the leopard catnaps. She is gracefully draped over my dresser. Occasionally she cracks an eyelid, smiles—yes, really smiles—yawns toothily, and resumes her napping.

Those are words I penciled onto the margin of a notebook when our leopard was thirteen months old, seventy inches long, and eating a two-and-a-half kilogram daily ration of ground buffalo meat, pabulum, and egg yolks. Such were the data I duly recorded at the request of a distinguished zoologist. Zoologists were interested in this cat, one of the few leopards (*Panthera pardus*) ever raised as a pet—and certainly the first to grow up in a city apartment with four teen-age youngsters. And so I kept records: empirical, factual, hopefully scientific. Only on the margins did I sometimes relax and turn my raw notes into a feline baby book.

"Leopards are more dangerous than tigers."

That specific warning came from several authorities and

I recorded it in my leopard ledger. Of all big cats, leopards have the most fearsome reputation. They are alert, lithe, and aggressive. Their intelligence is tremendous, and they can climb with far greater speed and agility than other large cats. Regarding wild leopards and those caged in zoos, there can be no rebuttal. Obviously, leopards can be dangerous. Yet my youngsters romped with our pet, took her for walks on the streets of New Delhi, India, and introduced her to rock music and their teen-age friends. We even put our pet to the test of family crisis—chaotic dinners, broken bones, one three-alarm fire, and a direct encounter with a wild leopard in a Himalayan village. The leopard passed each of those tests with utter loyalty and her own flair for high drama. If anyone failed, we were the ones. So today I turn the pages of my leopard book with nostalgic regret.

The story began, I suppose, long before we went to India. Perhaps my husband, Bob, though he seems too proper for such adventures, was really responsible for the leopard. Dr. Robert J. Davis, soil scientist with the United States Department of Agriculture, has always taken a more than tolerant view of my interest in animal life. We grew up together in Newark, Delaware, so that on our wedding day he already knew that I was a not entirely rational fancier of cats. And for twenty married years, Bob uncomplainingly shared our stateside homes with a succession of pets. Once he personally pushed me into the ownership of an exotic pet: he caught a wild baby skunk in George Washington National Forest. As soon as Bob picked him up, that young male answered forever the question of whether skunklings can spray. We called the newcomer Shalimar.

The children continued the family tradition. An attendant from a snake farm gave Jan a common water snake; it lolled on the dining room sideboard inhibiting the appetite of guests. We rescued a baby blue jay from one of our cats and fed him by hand so that he squawked for food whenever he saw me. A red salamander fattened on ants in a terrarium on the kitchen table while blue male betas and black mollies swam in Kristy's fishbowls. Our sons raised rabbits for Scout merit badges, white mice for a science fair, hamsters, and a South American caiman. Jan's white leghorn chicken shared my breakfast coffee.

Other creatures, if not pets in the usual sense, still joined our household as friendly neighbors. Two half-grown pileated woodpeckers, thrown from an overcrowded nest, adopted us and learned to sip water from a spoon. Squirrels took peanuts from our fingers, and mockingbirds begged us for raisins.

So our family included all those creatures who lived in our trees and raised their children in harmony with ours.

"When you get to India," knowing friends laughed, "you'll probably have tigers in your living room." I smiled. But I still recall Bob's uneasy response to that one:

"Well, I guess Rocky will do some such tomfool thing."

But first we settled our own problems of domestication in New Delhi. Ours was a family of four youngsters. Older son Rob, nineteen, had remained behind at the University of Illinois to major in fun. We would see him for summer holidays. The three junior members of the family were enrolled in the American International School in New Delhi: Rod, sixteen, a junior; Kristy, fourteen, a Titian-haired ninth-grader; and blonde Jan, twelve, in grade seven. We brought our house pets, of course—by now scaled down to two Persians, Nuyan and Baby Cat.

Disembarking at Delhi's Palam Aerodrome, we stepped into the steaming caldron of the Gangetic Plain in mid-monsoon. Our first impressions, like those of most westerners, were of heat and odor. It was a week before we could sort out the scents of India—acrid tar, carrion, dung, a compound of sharp pollens and heavy smoke.

We were assigned an attractive apartment in an old Muslim neighborhood near Nizam-ud-Din railway station. Our home sprawled over the second and third floors of a corner building; we even had a barsati, or roof garden, with a view of ancient, twisted neem trees arching over the street. And we could watch the pageant of life in timeless India. Down the dusty side street, young shrubs struggled for life in a losing battle against goat-herding squatters who raided for forage. Behind the houses across the street flowed the viscous nullah, part of Delhi's open sewage system, snaking its way toward India's second holiest river, the Jumna. From two blocks away, across Mathura Road in Nizam-ud-Din West, we could hear the muezzin's chant beckon the faithful to prayer five times each day.

Sipping our morning coffee on our front porch, we sniffed the pungent smoke of dung fires and watched the nationals and their animals flow past our home. Muslim families straggled toward the railway station after worshipping at the mosque behind St. Nizam-ud-Din's mausoleum. Humpshouldered cattle, dewlaps asway and goaded to a half-trot by eager herdsmen, hurried toward the grazing lowlands near the Jumna a mile away. Village women undulated toward the bazaar balancing on their heads wide shallow wicker trays heaped with dried dung patties, India's universal fuel. Scrawny sharp-nosed pye-dogs searched for food scraps in the litter dropped by succeeding waves of humanity. Across the street Khan Khanan's fifteenth-century tomb, architectural forerunner of the Taj Mahal, reared its desiccated dome above the tree tops, the rotting red sandstone bulk softened by luxuriant green shrubbery. And near us, on the grounds surrounding the monument, we watched our neighbors, bathrobe clad, sweat through their early morning calisthenics.

We hung draperies, hired two house servants, and visited the Taj Mahal. Bob and I both enrolled in Hindi classes. Then, as Bob settled into agricultural projects, the youngsters and I explored Delhi.

The Delhi Zoo made a special impression. It nestles beneath towering Moghul ruins of the Old Fort, a noble fourteenth-century backdrop for the gardenlike zoo itself: neatly graveled walks, precise flower beds, and broad lawns trimmed by mowers pulled by India's ubiquitous sacred cows. Each exhibit animal enjoys its own natural setting, usually behind moats rather than fences or bars. Mountain goats leap from rock to ledge on a miniature stone mountain, lions doze in two acres of scrub jungle, and tigers pad along game trails through spikes of elephant grass. Thanks to the local climate, the natural habitat of many species has been ingeniously duplicated. One has only to walk through this attractive zoo to feel a great respect for the people who run it.

Of course, we wanted to see tigers and leopards in their natural habitat, but postponed the idea. India's great wealth of wildlife is relentlessly being extinguished by the burgeoning human population, so the closest we could hope to find the large cats was in the Himalayan foothills. I returned instead to the zoo. And each time I passed the big cats—especially the tigers—I had an overwhelming desire to touch them just to see whether their coats were as soft as they appeared.

And then one balmy spring afternoon the Peace Corps opened the door to ownership of a big cat. Three Peace Corps volunteers, or PCVs, lived across the street from us, and because Bob and I missed our oldest son Rob, and because these PCVs liked our American food and air-conditioner, our living room had become a recreation center for the hungrier members of the Peace Corps.

One of them was Ralph Palmieri from Hammondton, New Jersey, who taught fifth-grade English in a New Delhi school. Lounging on our couch with a Coke in his hand, Ralph casually changed the course of our lives.

"One of my students," he said, "is named Predeep Sankhala. His father is director of Delhi Zoo."

"Really?" I said. "I'd like to talk to him."

Someone had told me that the zoo occasionally farmed out leopard cubs for raising—a kind of foster-pet project. But I didn't really want a leopard cub. "I'd like to raise a tiger," I confessed to Ralph. My daughters were listening.

"Mom! Are you serious?" Jan squealed.

"Would you really get a tiger?" yelled Kristy. Both girls could already see themselves parading down the street with a tiger on a leash.

"Certainly," I said.

"But what will Daddy say?"

"Oh, I don't think he'd be any great problem," I answered with more assurance than I felt.

Three months earlier, I recalled, when Jan had wanted to buy a dog with her Christmas money, Bob had said, "But this is India! I thought we were going to have *exotic* pets!" Jan had bought a dog anyway, but if Bob wanted exotic animals I wouldn't disappoint him.

Rod merely groaned. "Aw, Ralph! Mom just can't stay away from cats!"

Through his student, Ralph arranged my appointment with the zoo director. And so, on a March day, I met Ralph and Predeep at the gate and we descended the broad flight of steps into the zoo. Later I learned those steps were designed "to bring human beings down to the level of animals." I have reason to question the necessity.

As we entered his domain, Mr. Sankhala rose to greet us with a strong hand clasp. Tall for an Indian, he had a muscular frame and rugged good looks that reminded me of Johnny Weissmuller. "I am gratified," said Mr. Sankhala, "to find a westerner so deeply interested in our cats." Suddenly I felt as tense as a client in an adoption agency.

Over coffee, we discussed felines in general and in particular our mutual interest in tigers. I acknowledged that I knew almost nothing about them, but that their size and appearance delighted me. The director was pleased at honest admiration. He respects and loves his tigers with an objectivity seldom encountered in India and his knowledge of them is extraordinary. Abruptly, he interrupted our pleasantries. "Why do you want a tiger?" he asked.

Before this man, who daily walked with tigers, I could only stammer. I had raised domestic cats for twenty years, loved them, and understood their fine temperaments. To that extent, I thought I could succeed with a large cat. I even gargled up the idea that any cat with proper attention, regardless of size, should respond to affection. Mr. Sankhala left that assertion unanswered.

"Of course," he explained, "Delhi zoo never gives its animals to anyone. We never part with tigers at all except in unusual circumstances. However, if you want to purchase a tiger, the price for a golden Bengal is 6,000 rupees and for a Rewa white tiger 150,000 rupees."

Mr. Sankhala noted my stricken reaction.

"Fortunately," he said, "leopards are not so expensive. They reproduce easily in captivity, so every zoo has more leopards than we can use. Besides," he added, "leopards are far more difficult to handle than tigers. To raise a leopard would be a much greater accomplishment. . . . Would you be interested?"

I settled for a leopard there and then. Leopards, though only a third the size of tigers, are still big cats. It was an interesting challenge.

Mr. Sankhala mentioned a price of some three hundred rupees, and I couldn't argue. As soon as a litter was born, I would buy a leopard cub outright, thereby relieving Delhi Zoo of all responsibility. I was instructed to direct a letter to Mr. Sankhala stating my desire to purchase a leopard cub and promising not to turn it loose at a later date. In return the zoo promised to accept the animal once more when it should prove unsafe to keep in our home. All that remained was to await developments.

Obviously, Delhi Zoo entered into this contract not as a favor to me, but as a way to protect its own budget. If I failed to raise the cub, the young leopard would already have been paid for and the zoo would not lose an investment. On the other hand, if I were successful, the zoo had every reason to expect to gain a handsome cat reared at no expense to itself—no small item in an underdeveloped country where a zoo is sometimes considered a superfluous luxury.

The first fact of leopardology is that gestation takes ninety-five to a hundred days. Cubs were expected in early May and Mr. Sankhala felt one could safely be removed from its mother at fifteen days. If we visited the cub every day from birth, it would be accustomed to us before we took it home. Mr. Sankhala estimated that the first of June should be our Leopard Day.

"But bear this in mind, Mrs. Davis," the director cautioned. "The leopard will be safe for six months—possibly up to ten months. But positively no longer. Leopards have a cunning cruelty, and they are entirely unpredictable. Their dispositions limit the safety factor." He did not then mention the intelligence of leopards—either overlooking it or choosing to disregard it. In any case it is impossible to measure intelligence in a cage. "We quite honestly do not know the extent of domestication possible in leopards," Mr. Sankhala added. "Can you keep records for us?" It seemed that Delhi Zoo had attempted a similar experiment once before, but the young leopard was returned to the zoo in five months, physically stunted and neurotically confused.

"I certainly understand that this must be a short-term project," I heard myself say. "Parting will be difficult but necessary." Surely, I must have meant those things, but I didn't comprehend the size of the task I so blithely assumed. I had much to learn.

So did Bob. But there was no way to avoid telling the master of the house that he would soon share his castle with a leopard. After all, Bob only tolerated Nuyan and Baby Cat. As a precaution, I fed him a good dinner first, then told him all at once.

"The cub will cost three hundred rupees," I said, just to prove what a practical wife he had.

"Dirt cheap," said Bob. "Why didn't you order two?" He laughed, but he meant it. "Two cubs would keep each other company," he said, "and double the fun." Two would have doubled more than fun, but Bob had not yet faced the damage wrought by an only-child leopard. Dutifully—and gratefully—I wrote the zoo that the Davis family would accept more than one cub.

Oddly, our second son Rod, whose love for cats matches mine, seemed reticent. Perhaps he felt the time for jubilation would come after we had the leopard on our laps. Later, though, he and Rob delighted in inventing pranks designed to make me look silly.

"Why," asked Kristy, "does a cat have kittens, if a leopard has cubs? They're all felines."

The girls and I sought answers in Jim Corbett's books—long on entertainment but short on specific information. Kenneth Anderson's nature stories, we found, condemned leopards as cowards.

8

"Cowards!" said Jan with real indignation. "How can he say such a thing!" Already we were leopard partisans.

Sex worried us: which would be preferable? Males, because of their size, present a handling problem sooner; but females were said to be more aggressive. For hours we discussed suitable names. Horses named Smokey and dogs called Spot are usually inconsequential animals, so we discarded such names as unworthy. In the end we chose two names: for a male, Salim—a Muslim saint—and for a female, Sundari, Hindi for "the beautiful one." Cub or kitten, male or female, we would take whatever came, but we hoped for a female perhaps because we liked the name better.

One of our concerns was the old question, "What will the neighbors think?" But while we tried to judge the cub's effect on others, we couldn't anticipate the change in ourselves, nor could we conceive of the extent to which the cub would become attached to us. I tried to anticipate which people would be curious, which indulgent, and which would openly object. I knew neighbors in the United States would never put up with a leopard, but in India what goes on behind garden walls is a private affair and few will dare intervene. I reasoned that fear is born of the unknown and that if our neighbors saw the animal from infancy they, too, would enjoy it and raise few objections. Indians are invariably polite to foreigners; they truly want their guests to enjoy the country. I would rely on their hospitality and respect for privacy.

But what about our other pets? Adult cats should be able to control a baby, even one who outweighed them. Jan's puppy, however, had neither teeth nor claws for defense. He was less than a year old and we had saved him from a severe bout of scurvy after he had lost most of his teeth. Still, we were optimistic. Hadn't we raised so-called traditional enemies in harmony before? Affectionate discipline for all should ensure coexistence. But would it?

I had never been closer to a big cat than the safety rail of a zoo three times. Now I was spending hours in front of the leopard cages looking, just looking, as though proximity would impart insight into the nature of the beasts. Obviously, leopards were nervous animals, constantly pacing their cages. Even when they lay down, their tails flicked incessantly and they seemed always wary of unusual sights and sounds. Their sleek hides rippled softly with each movement; great chests and muscular legs showed their electric strength. The broad nose and wide-set eyes gave their faces a candid, benign expression. The roundness of their foreheads indicated to me a high intelligence. I could see nothing sinister in these magnificent creatures, only that they did not accept captivity in the placid way of tigers. I now compared the species: the tiger's very bulk lacked the fluid grace of the leopard. I wondered why I had ever considered tigers more beautiful and desirable. Stripes began to seem vulgar compared to the symmetric perfection of rosettes.

Mr. Sankhala, of course, still preferred his tigers, so I concealed my new loyalties. For the virtue of silence, I was rewarded one morning.

"You know our tigress Aseerfi?" the director asked. "Well, come." I followed as Mr. Sankhala strode to the cage of his favorite animal. I had to admit that Aseerfi was splendid: a mature tigress approaching five hundred pounds. She welcomed Mr. Sankhala with a soft, snuffling expulsion of air through her nostrils. He stepped close to the bars and reached inside the cage to scratch the great striped neck. Aseerfi stretched and luxuriated at the director's touch. He leaned closer and scruffed the light-colored belly of the tigress. She did not actually purr that time (though tigers do), but obviously Aseerfi thoroughly enjoyed the scratch.

"One must be careful, of course," said Mr. Sankhala. He explained that a single stroke of a tigress's paw can lop off a human head.

Time and again I watched Mr. Sankhala scratch Aseerfi. I took observant note of the director's stance and the way he rubbed the tigress. And then one day he turned to me, smiled, and said, "Would you care to try?"

Prudent Mr. Sankhala would never have suggested such a thing without complete confidence in the tigress and me. But was his confidence really justified in *me*? I could not tickle this tigress unless I stood within my own arm's length

10

of her. Was the risk of an arm really worth the dizzying thrill? It certainly was! So I eagerly—if cautiously—reached in to touch the smiling Aseerfi. The magnificent coat was not the soft plush texture I expected. The hair had a bristly feel and, beneath the loose, warm hide, the muscled strength of this great animal was awesome. She lolled happily, not caring who scratched her but only that it was done.

A number of times I scratched Aseerfi. At last—to my great excitement—she acknowledged my visits with her snuffling welcome sound.

Then on my regular visit to the zoo one morning an attendant asked, "Has memsaahib seen the keeper of tigers?" The attendant pointed to a man with a severely mauled arm. I recalled that he was one of the keepers who had seemed the most relaxed with his tigers. The sight of that man's arm put an end to my desire for further tiger tricks. Zoo tigers must never be considered harmless. They appear affectionate with their keepers, but beneath the calm manner they are fully as feral as their jungle kin. Their size, color, and magnificent manner never cease to thrill me. But the more I have learned about tigers, the more I hold them in respectful awe.

"In that case," Mr. Sankhala smiled, "perhaps you would not like to play with these tiger cubs." We made a hurried exception—Rod, Jan, Kristy, and I. And the tiger cubs, mischievously playful and cuddly, made us all the more eager for the young leopard we were awaiting.

Our friends and relatives took a less enthusiastic view.

I wrote Rob that when he arrived for his holidays we would bring a leopard to meet him at the airport. Rob's reply indicated some serious doubts about his visit. Then my Aunt Louise wrote that she had heard large cats had a vile stench. Our Hindi teacher insisted the beast would eat us all alive. "They start with your big toe and continue upward," she said. American friends remarked that at least we would have fewer house guests. Indian friends regaled us with gory descriptions of leopard leftovers. The tales provided us a delicious sense of superiority: we were the *nouveau* informed.

The month of May passed. On the first of June we still

11

had no leopard baby. There was nothing to do but assume that in time the law of nature would produce the cubs. I continued to watch the caged leopards. It was their eyes— those haunting eyes—that forced me to face an issue I had deliberately avoided. What possessed me to expose my children and pets to a beast of this sort? By what right did I assume I could defeat the feral instincts of a jungle predator? I didn't answer those questions because I couldn't. Yet I knew one thing: I wanted one leopard to view this world with eyes unclouded by fear. I wanted those magnificent lime-velvet eyes to look at me unafraid. Somehow I felt my love for a cat could accomplish the impossible.

2

EARLY-MORNING telephone calls have always annoyed me. And the June day was oppressively hot even at seven o'clock. Yet there stood our dark-faced bearer Murli, whispering through the bedroom door just loud enough to wake me and—he hoped—to leave Bob sleeping.

"Memsaahib? Phone call please, Memsaahib?"

I tried to finesse the summons by punching Bob with an elbow and keeping my eyes tightly squeezed shut.

"It's a phone call for you," Bob chuckled, knowing my curiosity would not permit me to stay abed long. So I arose, grumbling that the call had to be from an Indian because no civilized American would dare call before nine. The considerate Murli handed me a cup of coffee and I stumbled to the phone. Trying to light a cigarette one-handed, I picked up the receiver and grumbled, "Yes?"

"Mrs. Davis? Predeep Sankhala here. My father thought

you might like to know . . ." Predeep's Indianized Oxfordian English faintly penetrated the squawks and wheezes of Delhi's antiquated telephone system.

"Oh, uh, well, thanks, Predeep," I said, "I'll see what I can do about it." With the poor connection I could not quite grasp what he wanted, but it is always wise to be civil until the lines of communication are untangled.

"No, No!" shouted Predeep. "I said your LEOPARD CUB HAS BEEN BORN. If you will call at my father's office this morning you can see it." The words now jolted me to full consciousness.

"Wait, wait! Oh, Predeep, don't hang up!" I implored. "Please, is it a boy or a girl? Do you mean it? Is it really true?" The questions tumbled out.

"I think it is a female," Predeep hedged, "but it might be a male." His inborn Indian caution didn't allow him to commit himself to anything he could be called to defend later; he therewith hung up.

I sank into a chair, sipped some coffee, and finally got the right end of my cigarette lighted. The day now seemed historic; a scorchingly hot summer day in New Delhi, India, June 9; and our cub had been born. I wanted to dance, to sing, to shout from the housetops. And that, in fact, is exactly what I did.

Suddenly it seemed imperative that our Peace Corps friends should learn what a miracle they had helped produce. I couldn't phone Ralph because he had no phone. Nor could I dash across the street with my hair in rollers. So, taking the steps two at a time, I raced up to the barsati. I knew the boys would be asleep outdoors on the patio behind their house, so I bellowed across the street in full foghorn voice:

"Ralph, Bud, Jim! Wake up! I'm a leopard momma! Can you hear me? The leopard's been born. Come have coffee!"

Ralph, in skivvies and trying to rake sleep from his eyes, stumbled to the front lawn, and waved a feeble assent. A bit later, I checked on other neighbors. Little Mr. Chopra, sitting cross-legged on his verandah floor next door, kept right on shaving; he did not even bother to look up. The Sikh family

14

beside the Peace Corps house smiled a cheery good morning. The Singhs in the house on the other side of Mr. and Mrs. Chopra were breakfasting in the shade of their bougainvillaea; they nodded and put their heads together in a way that indicated one could not expect more of a foreigner.

Before I had noticed more reactions, Bob arrived on the scene. "The whole neighborhood doesn't need to know," he said. "Not at this hour!" I decided that Bob simply put an inordinate stress on decorum so I scurried to tell Rod.

"Yes, I've already heard," he told me. "So have people three blocks away."

Kristy and Jan, not so inhibited as the males of the family, shared my opinion that a new leopard was something to shout about. They were as anxious to see the cub as I, but since we didn't know zoo policy regarding newborn arrivals, we decided they should wait till later in the afternoon. I would first go alone.

Breakfast was gala. Ralph and Bud arrived, hungry and elated. We congratulated ourselves—Ralph for having discovered Predeep, all of us for our new arrival.

Not so the servants. The cook Hari and bearer Murli—both mahogany-hued Indians of untouchable status—served bacon and eggs along with their own anxious questions.

"*Kitnaa Baaraa?* How big, Memsaahib?" asked Hari. "Only *so* large?" He distrusted our airy descriptions, assuming anyone so unstable as to buy a leopard was an undependable source of information. Perhaps he was right: for not one of us had ever actually seen a newborn leopard cub.

By ten o'clock I had hied myself, camera in hand, to Mr. Sankhala's office. The director was polite as always, but on the whole blasé in the face of such a momentous event.

"A perfectly natural single birth," Mr. Sankhala assured me. "Without aid. The cub is small, but normal in all respects." Leopards usually produce two or three cubs per litter, but an only child was not unusual for this particular leopardess, Meenu. She herself was exceptionally small and rarely delivered more than one cub. The infant was indeed a female, so the name would be Sundari. "Very nice," Mr. Sank-

15

hala smiled, "The Beautiful One." As an interesting sidelight to Sundari's pedigree, the director added that Meenu had actually been the first animal in Delhi Zoo. Captured in the mountains of Kashmir, she had been presented to the board of governors by Jawaharlal Nehru, then prime minister of India, at an impressive opening ceremony.

Mr. Sankhala had left word that I should be admitted behind the outer security rail and could visit the cub whenever convenient. "So can the rest of your family," he added.

A sweltering sun was beating down from a cloudless sky. I can still recall the odor of cages not yet cleaned, but in a sprinter's time I covered the half mile between the zoo office and the leopard enclosure. Pleasant thoughts swirled through my mind. I pronounced the Hindi name aloud: *"Soon-duh-reé."* How gratifying that the zoo would consider the cub mine even though the sale would not be final until we took her home. I wasn't sorry there weren't more cubs, only happy this one had been born healthy.

The leopard keeper, a wiry black Indian named Budan, was prepared to humor an eccentric. A good thing it was, too, since he had plenty of opportunity in the next three weeks. He quickly moved Meenu into an adjoining cage and deftly fished the baby out between the bars. In the moment before he handed me Sundari, I drew my last objective breath about her. What is one's reaction to holding her first leopard baby? Mine at least was to hold her as close as possible. I knew no way to tell her she needn't be afraid, but my heart yearned for her to know. In that instant I realized she might never accept our family as her own. I tried to cuddle my beautiful lady but there just wasn't enough of her. My hands trembled. I could only think over and over, "Oh, dear God, she's mine." But I was wrong again: it was the other way around.

Sundari tipped the scales at nine ounces—approximately one generous cup of butter—on the scanty side for a newborn leopard. She showed little promise that day of ever living up to her name. Her coat, the consistency of a disreputable Teddy bear, had so many spots all running together that she looked as though she had just been fished from a monsoon

16

mud puddle. Her face, the size of a half dollar, was as wizened as that of a Pekingese, and only a faint squinchy line marked her eyes. Her head, minute ears pressed flat, was fetally long. Her body resembled a rat's. But like all animal infants, she was utterly irresistible. That wee blob showed a bravery she has long since abandoned, for she hissed at everything unfamiliar and struggled to escape the hands that imprisoned her.

Returned to her mother's custody, Sundari underwent the lavish laundering she deserved after consorting with humans. It seems an anomaly that leopards, usually so nervous in captivity, rarely fail to raise their young, while well-poised tigresses often ignore their offspring entirely or, worse, maim them. Sundari's mother was true to leopard tradition, and in all the times I saw her, she was ever gently maternal with her babe.

"Now be sure to keep her dry and be sure she's nursing properly," I told the leopard keeper. As I continued my instructions in English, he smiled uncomprehendingly. But with a desire to please, he wagged his head, in the way that signifies *yes* to Indians and *no* to westerners.

I had been so engrossed with the cub it wasn't until I reached the car that I remembered my camera still slung over my shoulder. But pictures didn't matter. I would be returning in a few minutes with the children. In fact, as I told the youngsters about Sundari, my enthusiasm snared even Rod.

"Do you think I could go back with you next time?" he asked. He couldn't believe her the paragon described, but when we placed Sundari in his palm, Rod went down without a fight. Rod Davis, aged seventeen, ring-a-ding leader of the American International School jet set, hard-shelled and soft-hearted, buried his nose in the tiny fuzzy body and sighed, "Mom? Oh, Mom, isn't she beautiful?"

I agreed with his sentiment, but not by the wildest stretch of imagination was that leopard beautiful—except in our eyes. Later Rod confessed that he had been unable to conceive of a leopard as anything but large and ferocious—and a threat to the life of our Persian cats.

Jan and Kristy and the Peace Corps boys visited Sundari

in the afternoon. They returned to say that, although I sometimes exaggerate, I had this time grossly understated the case.
Sundari was perfect.

Bob declined to see her. "I'll probably see more than
enough of her later," he said. "And besides, seven fools are
enough for any house."

We never arrived at a satisfactory explanation of Sundari's instant charisma. It couldn't have been pulchritude;
more likely it was that no matter how small and fetal in
appearance, she *was* a leopard. The very word strikes terror
in most people. But because Sundari was so tiny and defense-
less, she elicited fiercely protective emotions, maternal instincts in the girls and me, proud paternalism in the boys.

The keeper, Budan, was flattered by so much sudden
attention for his leopards. In the shadow of the great tigers,
his spotted beasts had never before caused such a stir; within
a few days he had become convinced that leopards really were
special. He proudly pointed out Sundari's older sister and her
father, and we prattled admiringly in a mixture of English
and Hindi. I worried that the June heat would be too great
for Sundari and that when monsoon rains began she might
catch cold on the bare cage floor. Budan had no control over
the weather, but he sympathized with us and shyly offered us
sweetmeats as consolation.

Then, seeing how much we admired his leopards, he felt
we would find even greater delight in his small daughter. So
the keeper brought his shy, dark child to the zoo for our
admiration. The little girl was just recovering from smallpox,
and yet I felt a pang of guilt that I could not stroke this
pitiful human child with the same joy I took in our cub.

Within a week Sundari no longer feared us and, in fact,
welcomed our handling. She quit trying to nosedive from our
hands, and instead snuggled into the curve of our necks—
a gesture that reduced all of us to jelly.

We visited the zoo daily—always once, more often twice
—usually with interested friends in tow. Everyone came away
enchanted. Bob, his curiosity getting the upper hand for once,

18

finally allowed himself to be persuaded to see her. I waited expectantly for his reaction.

"Well," he said, "for a two-week-old kitten, she's one hell of a big cat!"

I didn't ask him along anymore.

Traffic between Nizam-ud-Din East and the leopard enclosure of the zoo increased to such density that the keeper indicated, with Hindi and sign language, that he thought we should take Sundari home. Perhaps he felt our devotion should be rewarded, but more likely he had tired of the bother. Whenever our entourage arrived, Budan felt that he had to leap from his charpoy, or string cot, dispose of a drooping cigarette, assume a stance of importance, and be ready at all times in case we photographed him with Sundari.

As Sundari grew, her tiny head became rounder. Her eyes opened and gave her face an awakened expression of impish gaiety. The little body lost its rat look, and suddenly she could flick her three-inch tail in the manner of her forebears.

We recorded her progress on film. She was an accomplished model at an early age, calling up elfin expressions of pleasure, determination, or mischief all with the twist of a whisker or wink of an eye. She hammed before the camera as though she knew these were pictures for posterity.

Whenever two or more members of the family gathered, Sundari became the topic for discussion. Our letters to friends and relatives expanded to volumes describing Sundari's progress and behavior. In restrospect, the tones must have conveyed the idea India contained nothing but one young leopard. We wanted everyone to understand what a baby leopard was: harmless and heartwarming. It was important to us that, though they couldn't see her, they share our enjoyment of her.

On my visit one morning, I noticed a small but otherwise well-developed leopard in a cage behind the others. "Yes, this was the leopard returned to the zoo from the last experiment," an attendant told me. *"Bahut Kharab*—very bad." Further questioning revealed that the animal had been teased by the children of the family. At five months, it was undependable and dangerous. I studied the poor thing—obviously confused by its surroundings, its tormented eyes begging for release. While I stood nearby, the leopard came close to the bars and rubbed against them. Against good judgment, I reached in and stroked the spotted back. The animal seemed to relax under my hand. When I left, the poor thing whimpered.

That incident bothered me. I began to give serious thought to the consequences of taking Sundari out of the zoo milieu and raising her as something she was not. If Sundari was degraded to such a pitiable state through this experience, I could never justify it. Yet for Sundari, the Indian bush, not this zoo, was the natural habitat. Surely an affectionate home would give her a better life than a penal environment of cages.

On the fifteenth day of Sundari's life, Predeep called again. "The cub is progressing nicely," he told us, "but my father feels she is still too small to be removed from her mother." Mr. Sankhala would advise us later when we could take Sundari home. I was disappointed but I had to agree. The cub weighed less than two pounds; she would lose weight in the first few days before she accepted bottle feeding. We could not predict other results of the change in diet, but we had to face the possibility of stomach colic, diarrhea, or simple loss of appetite. A two-pound baby can't afford to lose two ounces.

Concerned over the feeding problem, I searched book stores and libraries for information. But I found only a dearth of fact and surfeit of fiction. The Bombay Historical Society, a reliable source of natural science materials, had nothing to offer beyond a small, unspecific item in its *Book of Indian Animals*. Popular works of Indian origin, usually written by British hunters, dealt more with the catching and killing of large cats than with rearing them at home. Mr. Sankhala admitted that although he knew about animals in the zoo, a cat in an apartment was another problem. "These are matters all of us need to learn," he said.

I consulted the veterinarian of the Delhi Zoo about diet

and care, but he was unable to assist. "You had better get a goat!" he said. When I asked why, he innocently inquired, "How else do you propose to assure a source of milk?" A goat in our roof garden, however, seemed like an overreaction.

I wrote our stateside vet for help. By airmail special delivery he replied that he knew nothing about leopards, small or large, except to avoid them. "But having doctored your dogs and mice, snakes and rabbits, newts and hamsters, cats and skunks," he wrote, "I don't suppose you would take my advice anyway. So I have forwarded your request to the National Zoological Park, Washington, D.C."

But even in Delhi, Sundari's fame was growing. Invited by Mr. Sankhala's office, a local newspaper ran a feature story on Sundari. We were reluctant to have our project publicized, partly because we were foreigners, partly because publicity might invite objections from fearful neighbors. But our worries were groundless. The headline read "Of Cubs and Carpets." And the story told about

> Sundari, three weeks old, about 18 inches long, wobbly on her feet and quite bewildered by the humans crowding into her new-found world. "Booked" months before her birth, Sundari will stay with her mother for another 10 days. After that she will go to an American lady who plans to rear her as a house pet.
>
> The process of getting the tiny cub used to her "foster mother" is going well. Mrs. Davis visits the Zoo every afternoon to play with her exotic buy. Sundari, on her part, is prepared to be friendly. Her most pantherish performance to date is an unimpressive "mew." . . .
>
> At present it is difficult to see anything attractive about the young feline, apart from her minuteness. Her fur is a dull muddy hue, her eyes bleary, her ears undecided whether to stand or fall. But Sundari bids fair to live up to her name before long. One day she will be 100 pounds of sleek grace with amber eyes and a glossy dappled coat.

When the story appeared, Rod spent half a day going from newsstand to newsstand buying up papers.

At the age of twenty-one days, Sundari could do little more than scrabble a few feet on wobbly legs. The legs themselves persisted in splaying out in all directions, giving her the appearance of a floundering turtle. Her eyes were now wide open and midnight blue, but of little visual use to her. She displayed the adventuresome daring typical of felines, a quality that has since brought her trouble more than once. While her mother napped in the shade, Sundari sought a wider world. No one knows how she hauled herself over a bar base three inches high, but she managed to enter the next cage— one belonging to her father, Mustahfa. Mustahfa sent her sprawling. When the keeper retrieved her, she had a two-inch gash in her shoulder and an injured left forepaw. Her two middle claws were nearly severed. How Budan saved her is a mystery, but, risking his own safety, he managed to scoop the cub out of the male's cage. Two sutures closed the shoulder wound, but for the tiny paw, no larger than my thumbnail, eight sutures were required. With a fat pressure bandage covering her left paw, Sundari looked like a one-fisted prize fighter.

She quickly recovered from the initial pain, recognized a theatrical prop when she saw one, and began to clown with the bandage. In our arms, she held it up with pride before the camera, and on the ground lifted it in mock distress.

Her mother, however, disapproved of the human devices. Daily the leopardess removed the fresh dressing as soon as possible, and as she bathed the baby, the mother's rough tongue loosened sutures and prevented proper healing.

"We are risking permanent damage this way," Mr. Sankhala told me four days after the accident. "I believe you should take the cub home to keep it away from the leopardess. If you are unable to feed the cub by bottle, then you can bring it back for a daily nursing."

I agreed to the suggestion, but privately I felt that so long as Sundari had ready access to her natural mother, she would never learn to rely on us. When she really made our home hers—and when she began to eat with us—the break should be complete. I raced home to pick up the carrying basket and to get Jan and Kris. They would want to be with Sundari on her first trip home.

In Mr. Sankhala's office to complete our transaction, the director went through a check-off list. "I want to ask that you weigh and measure the cub regularly," he said, "because no records of leopard growth are available here." We would keep an account of Sundari's growth, feeding arrangements, behavior, and abilities.

Turning to the financial settlement, I was distressed to learn that the price of leopards had risen. But how could I bargain over Sundari? I counted out the ransom, and Sundari was ours.

The girls and I walked out into the bright sunshine down the familiar steps toward the leopard pens. This time we could take Sundari home out of the rain and the heat.

Budan, in a burst of sentiment, seemed sorry to see her go. He followed us as we popped Sundari into the basket and started toward the car. I think he perceived that his moment of glory was past. In her brief stay with him, Sundari had stirred a flurry of excitement that Budan had never known before, a glint of glamour in a prosaic life. In that way, he was no different from the rest of us who have lived with Sundari.

3

THE BEST central location for Sundari seemed to be the coffee table in our living room, so there, with excited bustle, we placed her wicker basket.

All of us were tense, but the servants most of all. With a mixture of dread and eagerness, they ventured out of the kitchen: Hari, Murli, and the dhobi—laundry man—Ram Prashad. Each was trying to determine whether a leopard in the living room resembled in the slightest a leopard in the jungle. And each was ready for instant flight. Murli wore his shoes—a sure sign of impending departure—and Hari clutched his precious alarm clock, pressing the button down spastically so that the bell would not go off and enrage the beast. The dhobi straggled well behind the other two, ready to lead a disorderly retreat.

They halted just inside the door. Sundari was huddled down on the bath-towel bedding of her basket fortress. Her licorice-drop nose rested on the wicker rim and she tried to focus her myopic navy eyes in the direction of the new sounds; her ears—two tiny upside-down crescent moons—perched over a pixie face.

"You are sure, memsaahib?" asked Hari. I nodded. Murli meantime inched forward and made nervous clicking noises with his tongue. Tentatively he reached out a dark, gnarled finger to stroke the tiny head. Hari began to smile, but the dhobi, though he craned his neck for a better view, seemed to feel that his career had reached its nadir; he was working in a leopard house.

Sundari had already held many public audiences and knew instinctively how to captivate this delegation. She flourished her bandaged paw under their noses, sniffed their fingers, and returned their stares through bleary eyes. And thus she added three more men to her growing list of conquests.

But her charm fell short with her fellow animals. The two house cats—Nuyan and Baby Cat—were serene Persian adults, large and lazy, and they eyed any innovation with aversion. They were well aware Sundari posed a threat to the peace and quiet so recently established when they brought the dog to heel, and a new addition to the household meant renewal of their labors. From the first moments, they glared balefully, Nuyan from the back of the sofa and Baby Cat from the bookcase, their tails sweeping in great arcs of displeasure.

Panch, our half-grown Lhasa Apso puppy, showed far less poise. Bustling in from a romp on the barsati, he squeaked to an abrupt halt eye to eye with his new rival. For once, Panch didn't yap; instead, he peered quizzically through his facial fuzz examining the stranger—then retired to the front porch. Panch already had a six months' history of cat trouble. But he recognized Sundari as a vastly different development.

The servants returned to the kitchen. We could hear them laughing at their own fears and gossiping about the merits of working in a house with a leopard. Was Sundari really a leopard? Did the zoo know a leopard from a squirrel? If memsaahib was truly not mistaken, then all the lurid tales

25

they'd heard were told by false prophets; they, heroic servants, could spread enlightenment. *They* weren't afraid of a mere leopard. They could provide many an evening's eloquent entertainment for their cohorts. Some of their friends might work for saahibs of more exalted position, but no others could boast a leopard in their houses. Hari, Murli, and Ram Prashad were happy in their distinction. They would be happier still to pass on their harvest of leopard information. From that day forward, their affection and loyalty never wavered; they gave Sundari devoted, unquestioning allegiance. Their loyalty to Sundari made ours seem almost treacherous. We loved her in spite of her faults; they revered her without qualification.

While the girls padded a large cardboard carton with more towels, I switched off all our air-conditioners lest Sundari catch cold. The rest of us sweltered in the steam of July, but not one soul objected. We transferred Sundari to the packing crate so she could move about more freely. Then, when Hari called the cats for their evening meal, I was thunderstruck. With all my efforts to find out what to feed infant leopards, I had forgotten the implements to do so. I had no bottles or nipples.

Indian mothers still nurse their babies from the breast. While nursing bottles are available in some specialized pharmacies, they are not as readily available as in the United States. It could take hours to find a shop that stocked bottles. I had no close friends with babies, but finally the girls reminded me of a slight acquaintance who might have some used baby bottles. I instantly telephoned the lady. "For a . . . leopard?" she said with chill disgust. "I'm *terribly* sorry, but . . ."

My next call promised happier results; that friend had no bottles but thought she knew someone who did. In a few minutes more my phone rang.

"My name is Linda Kramer," said the voice, "and I hear you need baby bottles. I can let you have a few—provided you let me see that spotted baby of yours."

Linda lived nearby and promptly brought the bottles herself.

The formula was our next major problem. I hadn't prepared any baby formula for fifteen years, and I still had no firm advice from any practicing zoologists. I realized the risks of basing my mixture upon pediatric experience. Sauce for the goose might not work for the gosling. I had no idea how rich leopard milk might be, nor could I hope to duplicate it. The formula I decided upon was simple. Fortunately, Sundari thrived on it, and for as long as she nursed, we used the same recipe, changing only its quantity and concentration. The original composition was one part full strength Nestle's dehydrated whole milk to three parts Carnation dehydrated skim milk at full strength, one egg yolk, one tablespoon of light corn syrup, and ten drops multiple vitamins. I included the egg yolk for its protein value and discarded the albumin because of its adverse effect on the kidneys of some animals. Corn syrup was used for bowel regulation, and the vitamin drops were added because, well, because all babies should be vitamin-enriched.

I filled a new bottle to the three-ounce level and prepared to introduce Sundari to the scientific method of taking meals. The next half hour would have unnerved a gladiator. I was left bedraggled, besplattered, and lacerated; the cub remained in fine fettle. Baby leopards who do not wish to drink their milk from a bottle have distinct advantages over their wet nurses. They use carpet-tack teeth, tapestry-needle talons, threshing bodies, gyrating heads, and flailing tails. The nursemaid, terrified of hurting or choking her charge, focuses her attention on the worst gashes or punctures. The cub, equipped with a bear-trap jaw, slams it shut on intruding fingers.

I was distressed. Demoralized. And my howls of anguish testified to Sundari's determination. Her hide no longer resembled that of a secondhand Teddy bear. Now it was more like greased pig! When I finally gave up, I announced, "I don't want to wear Sundari out." But I was merely trying to cover up defeat at the paws of a three-pounder. Sundari herself was undaunted and indomitable. I was left to wash my wounds and to dread the next confrontation. Next time, I was telling myself, I'll don slacks and a long-sleeved shirt. At that moment Murli, having watched the Donnybrook from the kitchen door, came in bearing a plate of finely diced meat. He handed me the dish without a word, but his demeanor clearly expressed disapproval of my ignorance: everybody knows what leopards eat—and it's not milk! He was so sincere I couldn't hurt his feelings by refusing to take it. So when he had gone, I gave the cats a bonus meal. If all of us lasted so long, Murli would learn that leopards do drink milk.

At the next meal, we repeated the first performance—and broke a bottle. Sundari hooked the claws of both hind feet into my wrist and with a lusty shove sent the bottle skyrocketing. It hit the wall and shattered into a room-sized barrage of pyrex shrapnel and formula flak. Luckily, we were on the front porch where there was little to damage except my ego.

Sundari seemed to enjoy our brawls; she should have, since she won every round. And when the bouts were over, she snuggled down in my arms, triumphant. But I learned from each skirmish: I trimmed her toenails, thus reducing the odds. Deprived of eighteen potent weapons, Sundari found her defenses vulnerable. I now had only her teeth to contend with; and I called up reserves: Kristy pinned the squirming leopard to my lap and we succeeded in pouring two ounces of milk inside the kitten. When the joy of victory was denied her, Sundari quickly capitulated. By the end of her second day with us, she took the bottle willingly. By the third day she had twisted defeat into victory; her coquettish behavior had all the youngsters begging for the privilege of feeding her. Within a few more days, Sundari was pulling the bottle to herself with tiny paws and downing milk so fast that she gave herself hiccoughs. When hungry, she suckled someone's fingers. And by the time she was six weeks old, she padded out to the kitchen to ask for her bottle.

In the transition from zoo to home her weight loss was minimal. We fed Sundari on a demand schedule that was augmented by Murli. Almost hourly he appeared with a warm bottle saying Sundari was *"bhuukii,"* hungry. Telepathy is the only explanation for the way he knew because Murli was rarely in the same room with her for more than a few minutes. But each time Murli said *bhuukii,* Sundari was indeed *bhuukii.*

We recorded her formula intake after each feeding for six weeks; after that she seemed so well established we felt records unnecessary.

At first she consumed less than an ounce of formula at a time, but at the end of six weeks, she ingested five to six ounces at each meal. It was simple to improve the formula quality by slowly increasing the portion of whole milk and gradually decreasing the skim milk; the egg yolk, vitamin, and syrup content remained steady. We weighed the cub daily for a week to be sure she was not losing ground, but it should have been obvious she was not. Her tummy assumed the size and shape of an overinflated balloon; only her large, out-of-scale feet seemed heavy enough to keep this little living blimp from floating away.

Sundari was happiest cuddled in our arms. To simulate her mother's rough-tongue scrubbing, we gave her a rubdown with a damp washcloth after each meal. She rolled and smiled and patted at our hands as we massaged her little sides and flanks with the cloth. From the standpoint of cleanliness, these rubdowns were unnecessary, once she accepted the use of the bottle, but Sundari enjoyed them so much we couldn't deprive her of the pleasure. Constant licking by the mother, we reasoned, gives a cub a sense of security and also stimulates body processes, and while I wasn't sure our rubbings were accomplishing the same thing, I knew they couldn't hurt.

The first night I bedded Sundari in her box beside my bed. Bob was on an inspection trip to Hyderabad, so he was not there to object. Sundari herself made no objection. It seemed to me that if she was to depend on me as her mother, then she should be as close as she would have been to her physical parent. The next night I moved her onto the bed beside me.

The next night Bob returned to Delhi. When he saw the new sleeping arrangements, he had only one comment:

"You have put just about everything under the shining sun in my bed, but never—not even in my wildest nightmares—did I dream you'd put a leopard in our bed."

He was at least half serious. Bob, after all, was a farm

boy; animals were consigned to the barn. My outlook differed: nonfarmers have no business owning animals except for companionship. Pets should be in the home for enjoyment, and are thus an integral part of the family. It seemed unjust to lock them away at night. And so, until Sundari was more than a year old and her bulk grew too great, she slept with the two of us.

Sundari learned how to handle Bob as a bedfellow. As soon as he climbed into bed and pulled the covers up to his chin, she curled up on top of the covers, snuggling into the hollow between his legs. Bob was not only uncomfortable, he was also reluctant to move. "I don't want to wake up your cat," he muttered. That remained her favorite nightspot until she was too large to fit. Then she was forced to move to the middle of the bed.

"She takes up more than her third of this bed," Bob grumbled. He and I clung to each narrow side, fearful of falling out, not knowing the day would come when we'd be thankful if she just didn't stretch.

But although Bob continued to complain, he never failed to greet Sundari every time he came home. Time and again, he proved himself her grumpy, reluctant, devoted champion.

During her first eight days with us, Sundari returned to the zoo for the daily dressing of the injured paw. But I kept her strictly away from other animals because she might catch something—the beginning of my overprotectiveness. It didn't occur to me the zoo vet shared my isolationist views—for the same reason. The sutures were removed six days after the accident, but some residual infection still needed care. We had to keep the bandage so she would not lick off the medication and reopen the wound. Sutures had been torn out so many times by her mother that I worried over whether the paw would ever be normal, but when the gauze and tape were removed, the left paw worked as well as the right. The veterinarian had done a fine job. For several days the left paw seemed narrower than the other, but it soon spread out to match its mate; and by the time she was two months old, even the scars were hidden by soft fur.

During the day we put Sundari into the cardboard box for morning and afternoon siestas for her own comfort. She needed the seclusion its high sides offered. Felines often prefer to squeeze themselves into impossibly awkward niches for sleep. It is, I suppose, a carry-over from the wild state for protection against surprise attack, but within a week, Sundari was so much at home she dropped into a catnap whenever she happened to feel groggy.

Much of her day was spent in investigation, and she was soon quite at home in the front part of the house. But she could only see a distance of about two feet in front of her nose. The nose itself didn't work very well either; even adult leopards have a strictly limited sense of smell. Sundari groped blearily around the floor bumping into chair rungs and table legs, reminding us of a little old lady who'd lost her glasses. She stuck her nose into every nook it would fit and into every cranny it could reach, and within a few days she knew the layout of the living room and front porch. She especially loved to play hide and seek among the flower pots, hissing at the unwary puppy Panch, who beheld her in stark terror. Panch was completely subjugated, but she had less success with Nuyan and Baby Cat. She wasn't the first nuisance animal to intrude upon their serenity, and she wouldn't be the last. They might have their differences on other issues but were solidly united in their distaste for leopards, sniffing at her with noses held high and regal tails switching. No gangling, gimpy youngster could make them jump. Not yet.

Her horizons widened. She next explored the area between the living room and our bedroom: the kitchen, dining room, breakfast room, hall, and godown or storage area. In those regions she found a wide selection of amusements and edibles, and she began by supplementing her milk diet with servants' shoes, dustcloths, old newspapers, plastic sponges, a variety of mops and brooms, wooden mixing spoons, empty tin cans, full Coke bottles, and cardboard boxes. All these chewables she lugged into the living room for leisurely consumption.

At an early date she found that the lower kitchen cabinets

were excellent hiding places. She used them as launching pads for leaping at unsuspecting cats and caterers. She also tossed tinned goods out of the cabinets and she seemed to enjoy watching people who stepped on the cans and other obstructions. All of us developed the habit of walking head down—a hangdog posture—for constant ground surveillance. While one paw wore the boxing-glove bandage, we could keep track of her movements by the slish-slush sound it made on the bare terrazzo floor; when the wrapping was removed, she walked in dead silence.

But she could also make use of noise. Several nights after her arrival, we left the kitten in the living room while we went to dinner. As the vegetables were served, we heard an odd, staccato bark, not Panch's because he was with us. When I went to investigate, I found Sundari looking very pleased with herself. She had known where she was but not where we were. She smiled and wiggled her whiskers at me, and I knew she had added a new trick to her repertoire. Barking had worked admirably the first time and would be effective in future. And so she continued to bark whenever she wished to summon us.

It was at about this time that Sundari acquired her nickname. We began referring to her as the Cat. It was a term of endearment, as one would call a child by a pet name. We had cats but only one Cat. The others spoke to Sundari in English but I tried to use Hindi most of the time. I wanted her to be familiar with Hindi since most of the people she would meet would speak that language. She soon learned to respond whether she was called Pretty, a softer translation of her Hindi name than the formal "the beautiful one," or Sundari. In due time she learned to understand and respond to more than one hundred words in both languages.

Sundari had little difficulty following house rules, most of which she made up herself as the need arose. The few rules we laid down, she obeyed or ignored as she pleased. Toilet training was one of the rules she deemed worthy of disregard. I had strategically placed newspapers on the floors of all the rooms she frequented, but to no avail. Whether because she disliked the crinkly sound of the paper underfoot or whatever, she steadfastly refused to be coerced to use them. She even refused when we caught her in the act and moved her onto the papers. Had she been a dog or an ordinary cat I would have probably rubbed her nose in her accidents, but it seemed too great an indignity for a leopard. So I continued to hope that time would solve the problem. Eventually, she got the idea, but not until I had covered the noisy newspapers with bits of old sheets and ragged towels. When she did grasp the concept, she had trouble with marksmanship, for she sometimes put only her front paws on the paper. But we praised her anyway, telling ourselves it was the thought that counted.

The one sense Sundari possessed in high degree from the earliest days was hearing. She responded to any sound, however muted. If she couldn't identify it, she panicked and skittered for cover. Her half-moon ears were constantly perked for noise, and her vague eyesight compounded her fears. Soon, though, she learned to distinguish our footsteps from those of strangers, and she adjusted to normal house and street sounds. Her sense of hearing remained the most highly developed of her faculties; at one year she could distinguish the footfall of members of her family from a hundred yards away without seeing them. Her eyesight, almost nil when she was a small cub, rapidly improved; at eighteen months her eyesight rivaled her hearing. Zoologists have written that large cats generally have a poor sense of smell, and our experience confirms their opinion. Sundari never sniffed for her food; instead she looked and asked for it—or fetched it for herself.

Physical beauty is important to felines of all species, but much as she relished the bed baths we gave her, Sundari recognized us as incompetents. She made a fetish of cleanliness, toiling for hours at facials, pedicures, and the grooming of her tail. Soon she extended her preoccupation with hygiene to us. She awakened us every morning by washing our faces with her sandpaper tongue. Actually, it was a cheery way to start the day. I developed the habit of saying, "Oh, Sundari, leopard kisses are the very best!" She took this comment at face value and redoubled her efforts. For Sundari and me those words and those cheek-grating kisses became our greetings and good-byes, apologies and requests for attention, the expression of our mutual trust and affection. For all of us, Sundari's rasping baths served us in two ways: they improved our looks by leopard standards, giving us a permanent blush, and they rousted us out to play with her.

At age one month and three days, Sundari made her first public appearance when we took her to the airport to meet Rob, coming in from school. Big Bob was on tour in the Punjab when Rob's cable arrived, so the family reunion was incomplete. The chief customs officer took pity on me and gave permission for me to enter the inspection room. "You have not seen your son for a year!" he clucked. But the other children and Sundari had to wait outside the door in a milling crowd. After the first excited greetings, as we waited for Rob's luggage, I pointed to the doorway, "See, Rob? There's Kris with Sundari."

"Oh, Mom!" he scolded. "Why did you bring the leopard? Why not Nuyan or Baby Cat?"

"They've been here before and they didn't like it," I answered. But the customs man had overheard Rob.

"Whaaaaat! Where? Where? I don't see any leopard!" the official yelped. The word *leopard* carries high voltage in India.

"She's right there in my daughter's arms," I giggled.

"Do you call that a leopard?" Rob asked.

The customs man turned to look, relief flooding over him as he realized what sort of leopard Sundari was. He grinned. "I've never seen a leopard up close. Will you bring it in here?"

"She hasn't got a passport or visa," I teased.

"If I promise not to detain her, will you let me see her?" he smiled.

Kristy handed me Sundari and I placed her on the customs desk in front of the officer. A born actress knows how to play to each audience, and Sundari went into her vaudeville act like a trooper. She flopped on her back and waved all four paws in the air, then, regaining her feet, shuffled into a soft-paw routine. She stumbled in mid-routine and suddenly sat down to cover her goof. The officer was enchanted and called his cohorts to see the performer. The whole customs agency crowded around us to see and touch and smile at a leopard, and the cub received them as a queen her subjects, bestowing smiles in all directions. I have often wondered what other Delhi passengers must have thought as they waited for service in the torrid humidity of that July night. But Rob's passage through customs was unhampered by red tape that evening. "Do return," the man begged us, "and bring your leopard." But the other passengers seemed relieved when we left.

I don't know the exact moment our son Rob fell before Sundari's charm, but he cuddled her in his arms on the ride home from the airport. She licked his face. And she slept with him most of the next day when jet lag caught up with him. Two days later he either held her or was looking for her. And finally, the day she climbed a flight of steps looking for him, he became her willing slave. Never again did he mention his old, low opinion of leopards.

Gradually Sundari was developing her own language, a compound of various sounds in combination with facial expressions and body movements. She used her bark to call us, a high-pitched whine to indicate hunger, and a variety of grunts, groans, sniffs, and snorts to show pleasure or aversion. The most unusual sound in her vocabulary was a loud gulping swallow which meant either "Watch me" or "Look at that." It was a glottal stop I can only spell as *ulp*. She used it only to catch our attention for a specific thing in which she was interested. Her language was all her own, but we understood it perfectly.

For the first two weeks we kept our baby isolated from strangers, but we considered the PCVs and the children of our downstairs neighbors exceptions; they belonged. We weren't being stuffy, but we wanted to give Sundari time to adjust to her surroundings and to feel secure before outsiders came calling. At the end of that fortnight, her eyesight had improved considerably and so had her coordination. She could see clearly twenty feet and she scrambled up onto chairs with only a little help at the rear. She was still a clumsy kitten, bumbling along on stocky legs with a fat little belly scraping the floor for an hour after every meal; but her rate of growth

Sundari, at five weeks, playing Red Baron ready for takeoff. Charlotte Bush

was good, and her adjustment to the comforts of home was phenomenal. In many respects I underestimated her abilities. Yet she is the only animal I have ever known that convinced me she had an intellect—the power to reason. Throughout her stay with us her perceptive reactions were astonishing, and while it is true we tried never to ask too much of her, she never failed to measure up to our demands.

When guests arrived, Sundari invariably went underground until close monitoring proved her fears invalid. We always asked our friends to come in and be seated, knowing that Sundari's curiosity and her desire to be the center of attention would bring her out of hiding. A caller meant a new audience, and Sundari was always ready to go on stage. For openers, as a tiny kitten, she stumbled into the room as though she were *It* in a strenuous game of blindman's buff. Her creative acting focused all eyes right where she wanted them and brought murmurs of, "Oh, how sweet! Isn't she darling?"

With ladies it was an easy matter to paddle up to their legs as though to rub against them and then, with just the right amount of pressure, hook her claws into their nylons. During the uncomfortable silence that followed this trick, while the lady inspected her torn stockings, Sundari sized up any gentlemen in the crowd who might be snickering behind their drinks. She used a more athletic approach toward men. An unsuccessful, scrambling attempt to climb the seat alongside always made men feel very large and protective. They lent her a hand, and from there on it was clear climbing: straight to their shoulders where she licked their necks or hair. Now the ladies could laugh at the agonized grimaces and jumpy discomfiture of the men. If a show-off child had behaved so brazenly, everyone would have felt offended; but a leopard cub had license.

As she grew older, Sundari invented more parlor tricks, but she never pulled them on children. She sensed that to victimize a child was beyond the pale of respectability, so she remained content to tease adults. And her grown-up victims always returned for more.

Just as some people are cruel to animals, others behave inconsiderately. One mother brought her three rowdy children and made no protest at all when the youngsters started to shout at Sundari and tease her. I couldn't help but recall that pitiful leopard in the Delhi zoo, tormented by children into a state of confusion.

"I'm sorry," I told that mother. "You'll have to take your children home."

Another time a man came to the house and I tried to brief him. "Sudden noises frighten cubs," I explained. "So please try to avoid anything that will destroy her confidence."

Perhaps he didn't believe me, but at once he slapped the floor in front of Sundari's nose. Sundari's reaction was immediate and intense: she stood her ground, hissing and spitting. She was less than seven weeks old, and though she saw that man many times afterward, she always disliked him.

Yet I didn't want to keep Sundari away from people. I knew that the first few weeks would determine her lasting attitudes. I wanted her to see and meet as many people as possible so she would know there was nothing to fear. Bob and I talked it over and worked out some house rules: no one would be allowed to come into the house unless Bob or I was present, and no child under ten would be admitted without a responsible adult. A few special friends of the children were excepted—those we knew well. But we enforced the rules strictly with casual, curious visitors who'd simply wanted to see a leopard—and there were many of them.

Just after Sundari was six weeks old, I awoke one night—about two o'clock—to find her gone from the bedroom. I searched in closets and under furniture—no Sundari. Widening my search, I tried the bathroom, godown, and hall and worked my way toward the front rooms. I couldn't imagine what had become of her, and was about to rouse the household, when Kristy called, "Is that you, Mom? Are you looking for the Cat?"

"Yes," I said, "How did you know?"

Kris opened her door and stood leaning against it sleepily grinning at me. "I heard her barking at my door a while ago so I let her in. She just wanted someone to play with her, but now she's asleep on my bed. Do you want her?"

"Not if you do. I was just worried," I answered, and straggled back to bed. This was our introduction to Sundari's early hour revels and what Bob called our midnight madness. The Cat regularly awoke anytime between midnight and three o'clock—not hungry, but ready for games. It wasn't too strenuous an exercise when she was tiny; I found I could lie in bed, half asleep, and wiggle a finger or toe for her to pounce on. But as she got older, Sundari became a nightly nuisance. In order for any of us to get a full night's rest, we had to take turns amusing Sundari for an hour or so. Unfortunately, Sundari wasn't always aware whose turn it was and whose turn it wasn't. The arguments were resolved when the school year began for Rod, Kris, and Jan. All night duty devolved entirely upon Rob and me. Bob, of course, refused to budge from his bed.

We didn't turn Sundari into a nocturnal sport. In simple fact, we shaped her hardly at all. We only gave her the atmosphere for her own expression. Her charm lay within. She was a happy, carefree kitten—outgoing, friendly, and always entertaining. Not once did she exhibit the sly, cunning traits so often associated with her species. That she loved us was obvious from the beginning, and she displayed her affection continuously—rubbing against our legs, licking our hands and faces, butting us with her head, nuzzling our necks, burrowing herself fondly into our laps. At first, we had been attracted to the idea of owning a leopard, but even before she entered our home she had entered our hearts. We loved the animal, not an idea. Her intelligence, her sensitiveness, her personality, and her pleasure in our company combined to bind us to her in ways transcending an owner-pet relationship. For me she was a good companion; for the other animals, a playmate; for the servants, a useful accessory after the fact; for the children, an accomplice; and for Bob—now and again—the bane of his existence. She was a spotted sorceress, and her charms held us spellbound.

4

AS A bulky, six-pound cub, Sundari needed a playmate. So she turned to the dog Panch, our shaggy, seven-pound Lhasa Apso from Tibet. Panch responded with tentative paw-jabbing feints and a timid yap that scared Sundari under my bed. But when she emerged, Panch was waiting for her, and at that instant they became partners in a demolition project that lasted for weeks. Their activities required Murli's full-time attention sweeping up, sopping up, picking up, patching up.

The leopard and the Lhasa Apso caroused drunkenly through the house, under foot and over furniture, through clusters of guests and pots of philodendron. They scrounged in clothes hampers to get ropes for tug-of-war, played Tarzan on tablecloth corners, and more than once draped toilet paper streamers from the bath to the breakfast room. They rummaged in our closets to find new toys. They played kick-the-can; home base was inside a kitchen cabinet. They smashed flower pots,

scattered the dirt, and ate up the wilted blooms. They raced
to see who could chew through lamp cords first. They even
devised a form of drag-race chicken: starting at opposite ends
of the apartment, they charged toward each other and met in
a mighty crash—skull to skull. Between such diversions, they
wrestled each other and, when exhausted, collapsed just long
enough to gather strength for the next orgy.

Panch had never had so much fun. Nuyan and Baby Cat
considered him a pariah, and until Sundari introduced him to
the delights of deviltry, he had done nothing more offensive
than bark at strangers. With the spotted cub's encouragement,
the innocent, tongue-lolling pup found sinful inspiration. He
soon taught Sundari how to dig in the sand of the cat litter
box. And with one flat-pawed swipe the cub learned to spray
sand fifteen feet. Our storeroom began to resemble a Sahara
shanty.

Sundari reciprocated. She introduced Panch to the pleasures of cat-baiting, and she cleverly used him as the decoy
while she nipped the rears of the house cats. Such games
turned Nuyan and Baby Cat from their elegant, slit-eyed
complacency into a state of claw-slapping, tail-snapping, fiery-
eyed ire.

We gazed at the wreckage in disbelieving fascination.
Such havoc just didn't seem possible. But the inventiveness of
the pair was boundless. And once Sundari learned to open
doors, the last of our family privacy vanished.

"What is your husband's reaction to this mess?" a shocked
friend once asked me.

"So far, we've hidden it from Bob," I said wanly.

After all, our saahib was always gone during the day, and
more often his work was taking him on tours away from New
Delhi. He had been a good sport about the leopard project, but
as Bob himself had said, "Just remember—the cat is all yours."
The rest of us, though, found the cub and the pup so engaging
that we forgave them everything. When our truants tired, they
dozed in a single tangled mass of paws, fur, and tails. How
could we bear a grudge?

Early in their association, Sundari developed the habit

of curling up between Panch's legs, nestling her little body against his pudgy stomach. But Panch had already attained his full growth and Sundari had not. In a few weeks she was unable to fit into her sleeping place, but she couldn't understand why. For weeks she tried positions anterior, underneath, and on top of the little dog in futile attempts to wedge herself into the protective custody of his stubby legs and body. Finally, unable to recapture the past, she settled for wrapping herself around him, thus reversing their original napping posture.

Sundari found only one major fault in her friend: his perpetual need of a bath. Panch had a truly Tibetan horror of water, and although Jan bathed him regularly, Sundari wasn't satisfied. The leopard spent hours licking the dog. He never enjoyed the washing, but he seemed to accept his baths as the price of her companionship. Still Sundari never quite succeeded in grooming the pup; his long hair forever fell in his eyes, and he yelped whenever the barbs on her tongue pulled too hard on the snarls of his coat.

Panch's yelp, in fact, was a sure defense against the rough play of his powerful pal. The shrill sound hurt Sundari's ears and always sent her scurrying into retreat. And the roughhouse play would turn toward furniture. Not even the faithful Murli could keep up with the damage of the growing cub and pup. Sooner or later, I knew Bob would discover the truth. Somehow, I knew we had to separate the pair.

Then, unexpectedly, a Peace Corps friend was transferred back to the United States. "My parents own a kennel," she told us. "And they want to raise Lhasa Apsos. If you'll send Panch to them they'll save one of his pups for you." All we had to do was provide Panch with certified rabies shots. Since it was also time for the semiannual shots and checkup in our whole animal household, I called Dr. K., a New Delhi veterinarian, for a wholesale appointment. We first discussed Panch, Nuyan, and Baby Cat. Then I brought up the larger matter.

"I have a leopard cub, too," I said. "Will you take care of her for me?"

For a moment, I thought the telephone had been disconnected. Then the vet's voice came back, though hesitantly: "Yes, but what do you want done?"

"Just a routine checkup," I said, "and perhaps a worming. I'd like to bring her along with the others."

"That will be fine," he said. "Bring them along any time between five and seven this evening."

I had the impression Dr. K. didn't know what I had, but he certainly didn't think I had a leopard. He probably thought I had bought some kind of animal from a fraudulent peddler.

Four animals, even with five people to handle them, can be a chore to transport, so I asked a friend to drive us. That freed me to hang on to Sundari; I distributed the two cats and one dog among the four children. The weather didn't help; we set out in a July monsoon downpour. The cats were damp and annoyed; Sundari made snuffling grunts and Panch was too cowed by the commotion to make any sound at all. I lost all hope when a tire went flat, but the station wagon limped to the curb right in front of the vet's office. Through the monsoon, we lugged our menagerie inside.

As we entered the waiting room, a voice called out from behind a partition, "Mrs. Davis? You *do* have a leopard! I can smell it!"

I sat down and did my best to smell a leopard, but the only odor I could sniff was a slightly milky smell from her last bottle. I couldn't help laughing when Dr. K. appeared and said, "I didn't think you really had one."

"You've lots of company," I said, "but you're the first to identify her by smell. How can you do it?"

"If you weren't with her all the time you could tell the difference," he replied.

Maybe he could, but I couldn't. I have sniffed at Sundari before baths and after; in the morning and at night; before, during, and following her meals—and I have yet to detect an odor about her other than a faintly dusty but not unpleasant scent on her paws.

Dr. K. quickly and deftly gave the rabies injections to Nuyan, Baby Cat, and Panch, but he approached Sundari in a gingerly fashion. If he hesitated to touch a cuddly cub, I wondered, how could he handle her later? Actually, I don't think he was particularly afraid of her at that moment, but his mind's eye was projecting the future. Veterinarians with a practice among small animals do not expect to face patients like Sundari. And since they see the animal infrequently, they have no opportunity to establish the rapport so necessary with pets of undomesticated species.

Dr. K. gave Sundari a tense examination. "She seems in good health," he said. "But we should probably worm her as a general precaution." He produced a worm pill—clutched in ten-inch tongs like a hot coal. Then an assistant appeared to hold the victim. Indian vets never want aid from owners but insist that a low caste, usually dirty youngster assist by grasping the patient's legs and body. This assistant was both clumsy and scared.

Perhaps I should have been more understanding. After all, in the old India of even a few decades ago, medical doctors never put their hands upon a patient, since the Brahmin practitioner would have been defiled by the physical contact. But I couldn't take time to reason: Sundari was blindly terrified of the grappling, poking strangers.

"This is ridiculous!" I heard myself say. "Give me that pill!"

Cradling the baby leopard in my arms, I let her suckle my finger; in a few seconds, I withdrew it. She opened her mouth to recapture the comforting finger—and in popped the pill. Then she dutifully swallowed.

My visit to Dr. K. taught me a most important lesson: eventually, I would have to assume the full responsibility for doctoring Sundari. With strangers, leopards have a curiosity that equips them to make friends easily. But leopards are also shy, nervous, and so sensitive they know at once how individuals regard them; the smallest indication of fear or distrust, either by glance or manner, makes them instantly wary. If vets fear an animal, they have two choices: to dope the animal heavily or to use a squeeze cage as zoos do; neither treatment is desirable for pets. In emergencies, there isn't time for sedation.

And a squeeze cage could terrify any pet—bars closing like jaws to pin the animal. A pet could certainly associate the experience with humankind generally and might never regain confidence in people.

So from that day on, I sought the best medical advice I could get and administered all of it—from pills to shots— myself. Luckily, we never had an emergency.

The zesty Panch departed India by air in a handsome aluminum cat-size kennel. Sundari did not see her playmate off, but during the next weeks, she missed Panch poignantly. For hours on end, she searched the house for him, returning time and again to all Panch's favorite hiding places. Then, dejectedly, she would come to me and gargle some throaty, conversational noises to tell me that Panch was still missing.

The other feline members of the family proved poor substitutes in Sundari's life. Nuyan and Baby Cat maintained a stolid, aloof attitude except when Sundari tormented them. Then they assumed the watchful mien of Minutemen ready to defend home and hearth against all comers. To the house cats, the leopard was an interloper on the peaceful domestic scene. As city dwellers, they didn't know they should be afraid of their country cousin. At first, they resisted every overture from Sundari, whether peaceful or prankish. When irritated, they served her claw-distended clouts which sent the cub skittering for my bed. There, snuggling in security, she would wash her face for comfort. So Sundari learned to respect the house cats the hard way, and long before she was large enough to harm them, found they left her alone as long as she stayed out of their way. Her respect gradually turned to admiration and even affection—though she gave up the brawling life she had known with Panch.

When Sundari began to play with Panch's old toys, we realized that she needed some of her own. So we started her collection of playthings. First we got her some plastic squeak toys, among them her favorite, a yellow and red fish. Sundari objected only to its noise, so she performed a neat squeak-ectomy. She took such good care of the fish that it was still in active service seventeen months later.

45

In all her playthings and surroundings she was drawn to bright colors: red most of all, and yellow next. She adopted a bright green overstuffed armchair as her own and, when not sleeping in it, hiding behind it, or playing treetop on its back, she used it like chewing gum, gnawing endlessly on its nether side.

Her greatest treasures were plundered from the closets. Jan, for example, had a pair of soft nylon knee socks with flabby elastic tops; we padded them with scraps of cloth, then knotted the tops. Then we left the stuffed socks in inconspicuous places—inside the stereo speakers or behind the refrigerator—because Sundari had more fun if she thought she had stolen them. We ghoulishly dubbed these socks her "legs." She loved them. She lugged them to the barsati—and to bed; she hid them behind potted plants and hauled them to the backs of chairs, and she always knew exactly where they were. We laughed at her efforts to drag them when she was still small. With her head held so high she couldn't possibly see where she was going and the "leg" dangling between her forepaws, she tripped time and again.

Half-gallon plastic Clorox jugs proved almost as durable. Carefully washed, the jugs provided her more hours of enjoyment than any other items in her toy chest. The dhobi Ram Prashad provided Sundari an ample supply—at what cost to our clothes I am unwilling to admit. She carried the jugs to the tops of almirahs and bombed us as we sought clean clothes. She carted them to the top floor to drop them three flights down the stairwell with resounding clatter, and she nursed each jug until it was shredded or until we gave her a new one.

Each weekday Bob and I met at the embassy for our lessons in Hindi lasting from one until two o'clock. Trying to beat the heat, I always bathed just before leaving, and it was Sundari's habit to watch me from a perch atop the closed toilet lid. She always sat on her throne elegantly, her brow creased with interest.

One muggy August afternoon I had filled the tub with ten inches of tepid water and was lathering myself when she cocked her head to one side and leaned forward for a better

Rocky introduces nine-week-old Sundari to an artificial "leg."
Charlotte Bush

view. Perhaps I wiggled my toes; at any rate, the next thing I knew, paws akimbo and tail aimed skyward, nine pounds of spotted fuzz launched itself into space. What began as a swan dive ended in a belly flop. Geysers of water soared high. Waves engulfed me. Sundari was spluttering from surprise—and so was I. Suddenly I realized that the cub could drown, and I grasped her by the nape of the neck and hauled her head out. Indian bathtubs are narrow, slick, round-bottomed and high-sided. They can be tricky for maneuver in the best of circumstances; when rescuing a leopard, such a tub is little short of dangerous. But, hanging onto the slippery cub, I grabbed a towel and got us both out and, trailing rivulets of water, placed her on my bed for drying down. I began to laugh. A drop of water on the tip of each whisker made Sundari's mustaches droop like those of a foiled villain. Her nose was wrinkled in disgust, and the wet fur plastered to her body accentuated her midriff bulge. She told me in throaty rumbles that tub baths were terrible—or so I thought. Leopards were supposed to despise water, so I felt sure she had learned her lesson. How wrong I was!

The next day Sundari jumped into the tub before I got there. She has been taking baths ever since. She prefers her tub warm, and well populated with people and toys! We even had to warn house guests to lock their doors before running water, and I made the children promise to keep their water level below eight inches. When it was inconvenient for Sundari to join us in her entirety—such as at her mealtimes—she treated us to reproachful looks, but came running to hang over the sides to dabble forepaws in the water. If nothing else, we had the cleanest leopard in town. And perhaps the cleanest floors, since Murli was forever mopping up behind her.

As our cub grew, we watched her shed baby fur. Then her feeding routine changed. Taking her bottle, she sometimes let the thing dangle from her lips like a five-cent cigar; other times she balanced the bottle with two paws or peddled it with four. Halfway through a meal, she would stage love-ins with the feeder, and we would have to fend off milky kisses. We attributed her attachment to the bottle in part to her enjoyment of cuddling, but no one needed to tell me she should be eating meat. She began gnawing through nipples at a rapid clip and she asked for her bottle too often. Her formula had been strengthened with more egg yolk, but she refused to lap Pablum cereal from a dish. So I asked Mr. Sankhala for his advice.

"Try liver," he said.

We bought half a pound of calves' liver and presented it to our leopard. She took one look and walked off with her nose in the air. Sundari, like all felines, disliked novel ideas unless they were her own, and her attitude toward meat was that we were serving her a plate of Paris green. I tried every approach short of sharing it with her. When I rubbed liver on her paws, she danced around as though someone had dropped her on a bed of hot coals; she quite refused to lick it off. When I tossed bits of liver across the room, she looked at me as if I had lost my wits. Raw or cooked, diced or whole, morning or evening, Sundari would have none of it. Yet each day her hunger was growing. She showed the same disdain toward chicken and goat's liver. In the wild, cubs learn to eat meat by lapping at their mother's dinner, but I wasn't about to eat liver for Sundari—raw, cooked, or any other way. I happen to despise liver myself. Now, I wonder if my own aversion had anything to do with Sundari's. Even at nineteen months, Sundari still refused liver.

Awake and asleep I mulled the problem over. Finally, I came up with the idea of adding strained baby meat to her milk formula. The meat would dissolve, and if we enlarged the holes in the nipple the slightly viscous fluid could pass through. Up to a point, my reasoning was sound, but that point was at Sundari's mouth. She was comfortably ensconced on my lap and prepared for the delights of the bottle, when she discovered my ruse. Insulted to the core, she sulked for two hours under my bed. After that, she spent another two hours messing in the kitchen, and I mean just that. She delved into the cabinets to rearrange the contents, overturned the garbage can and slopped its contents on the floor, climbed to the counters and smacked off every movable object, and finally came to rest in the sink from which she refused to be moved.

49

In desperation Hari called me: "Memsaahib? Please to come to get Sundari?"

Determined to get the better of her for once, I deliberately poured six ounces of formula into her bottle and added two teaspoons of baby lamb. Then I warmed the bottle and waved it under her nose. "Come on," I said, and she came—she was too hungry not to, but she argued all the way, dragging her paws in dissatisfaction. She clambered onto my lap grumbling. Then with some feeling I said to her, "You don't want this bottle? You can take it or do without! It's up to you, Sundari, this is the end!"

Her nose was wrinkled in distaste and her whiskers laid against her muzzle, but she could no longer avoid the problem. With a deep sigh of resignation, she tried one little sip. She didn't drop dead as she had perhaps feared, but she stopped to tell me it tasted terrible, then she fell to with a will.

Encouraged by this success, I hit upon another ruse: I smeared my face with strained lamb baby food, then presented it to be washed by the fastidious feline. Sundari swallowed hook, line, sinker, and lamb. It was probably the only time that my Cat was ever outwitted. She couldn't resist a dirty face, but I hate to think what the embassy medical officer would have thought had he seen me during the next week. We improved Sundari's diet at some cost to our human dignity. I tried another trick, offering meaty fingers instead of my cheeks; by that time, she was accustomed to the taste of lamb, so fingers worked, too. Then, while she was busy washing my hand, I slipped a dish of meat under her mouth and removed the hand; before she had a chance to protest, she was lapping food from the plate. But Sandari had one stopping point: she might be conned into eating from a dish; but no one, man or beast, was going to make her believe leopards dined on the floor. For the next month we had to hold her in our laps while she ate breakfast, lunch, and dinner from a hand-held dish.

Even at the time, I knew I was behaving like a fool with Sundari. Had I wished, I could have forced her to do my will, but why do things the hard way when fun is possible? When my own children were small I was a strict mother because the

50

youngsters had to learn to live in harmony with people; but with Sundari I had turned permissive: people would have to learn to live with her. So Sundari was the child I could spoil, the tot I didn't have to punish, the amusing little one who could do no wrong.

Once sold on solid foods, Sundari enjoyed the tangy flavor, and we introduced her to boiled ground buffalo mixed with baby cereals. Other than her formula the staple food of her diet continued to be cooked ground buffalo. We cooked the meat not because we were afraid that raw meat would excite our pet, but to destroy parasites which are ever present in subtropical lands. The meat was ground up because that was the way we fed it to our little cats; it was easier to have all pets eating the same thing. I should like to mention that I reject the myth that predatory animals get a taste for blood from raw meat. Had it been convenient to feed Sundari raw meat, I should have done so without any reservations. Raw meat would no more have inspired her to attack us than it does wild cubs to attack their litter mates.

Each morning Sundari got a ration of meat mixed with Pablum cereal, two egg yolks, and twenty drops of multivitamins; in the evening she had another bowl of meat mixed with one jar of baby lamb, veal, chicken, or pork; later, calcium was added. The baby meats were simply for flavor to prevent her tiring of the same tastes day after day. One leopardologist has stated that leopards cannot be raised on a diet of buffalo, and I have tried to understand his reasoning. Sundari has not only survived but thrived on it. The protein value of all meats is essentially the same, so it should not matter whether the leopard eats goats, chickens, dogs, or buffalo. The egg and vitamins and strained baby foods and calcium provided the best possible diet.

I am told leopards normally eat once a day, but Sundari was fed solid foods three times daily with two additional bottles until she was four months old. Then she ate two meals a day. She continued her bottles until she was five months, when she bit the top from our last nipple. Boiled water was always available for our animals, as was a dish of dry cat chow for snacking. Most zoos observe one fast day a week on the theory that felines do not necessarily eat every day in the wild. I could see no reason to follow that procedure.

While we were still experimenting with Sundari's diet, I received a long letter from Mrs. Janet Davis, medical technician at the zoo of Washington, D.C. Mrs. Davis was answering an emergency plea for help that I had written weeks before. She approved the milk formula, and agreed with Mr. Sankhala that Sundari should be eating meat. Mrs. Davis suggested live white rats or healthy young chickens as a good beginning. I could think of nothing more plentiful in India than rats but none I had seen were white; and the Indian chickens available at our markets were sickly and poor. Zoos normally feed raw meat and leopards obviously don't cook in the jungle. But all things are relative, and after weighing the dangers of serious infection and worm infestations, we stuck with boiling. We always saved the pot liquor from the cooking pan and used it to moisten Sundari's morning cereal so that we lost little or no nutritive value from the meat.

Mrs. Davis also recommended giving a tablespoon of calcium carbonate each day and a vitamin compound not available on the Indian market. Though we made substitutions, we were on the right track. So, encouraged by Mrs. Davis, my confidence grew.

Sundari's special meals brought one side effect: Nuyan and Baby Cat, sniffing the delicacies, flew a flag of truce. By the time Sundari started with solid food, the two little cats had already so impressed the cub with their exalted importance that Sundari would not have dared put her nose in their dish —one of the leopard's few inhibitions. But on the day Sundari's food was placed on the floor, those two cats lost their anti-leopard prejudice. Poor Sundari didn't know what to make of their sudden friendship. She was hungry as they, but had learned her lesson so well she would not crowd them. So I actually had to teach that leopard how to scrabble with two little cats for her food. I held back the cats until Sundari began eating, then, when her head was in the dish, I released them. By then, they couldn't budge her. Before long I decided if they were going to get her meals and their own, too, we might just as well put it all together—theoretically the largest mouth would get the most meat. We put their food in nine-by-thirteen-inch cake pans so Sundari had room for her broad nose beside their little heads. Even at twenty months, Sundari still refused to force Nuyan and Baby Cat from their meat, sharing her food with them—even when she had gone hungry for as long as four days. I have never heard Sundari warn them off in any way. But when she thought they were getting the lion's share, she would pull the pan toward herself with a very tentative paw—a gesture that never bothered them. The little cats just skittered along with the pan, scarcely raising their heads. When her head was as large as their whole bodies, she would not nudge them aside, but patiently waited for them to make room for her. If the waiting period proved overlong, the leopard bathed the house cats while they ate. It has always seemed to me that Sundari's willingness to share her food with the cats and dog was a good indication of her emotional stability and the strength of her attachment to those around her.

The Persian epicureans could hardly continue to despise their hostess, so a new era of feline togetherness began. Sundari was so pleased with their acceptance that she laundered them whenever they permitted. Baby Cat relaxed his vigilance to the point of playing with her; he was little more than a kitten himself. But though Nuyan, an old man of two years, ate with Sundari and sometimes slept with her, he wouldn't join her rollicking games. Instead they taught the leopard the old art of begging at the dining-room table. Nuyan and Baby Cat were masters at the art, and Sundari, the wittiest of the lot, was an apt apprentice. She quickly figured out who got the choicest tidbits. A born mimic, Sundari had no trouble imitating the floppy-whiskered, droopy-eared, and wide-eyed look of her teachers; and with her rubbery face she could achieve a sadder expression than they. She tried to follow their techniques: a soft tail barely dusting across the diner's legs, a gentle paw on thighs; and if those overtures didn't work, she could try a little—very little—claw. If all else failed, one placed both paws on a thigh and slowly rose to stand on hind legs and peer at the heaped plate of the diner. Quick as she was, Sundari had two handicaps with the mendicant arts.

From left to right, Nuyan, Baby Cat, and Sundari, at eighteen months, share a bite of food. Davis

Her tail-work under the table was never very good; she lacked the plumage, and at three months she used her tail more like a bullwhip than a feather duster. Her second problem was of greater consequence: her size. Nuyan and Baby Cat, when stretched upright, only rested noses on the edge of the table; but a standing Sundari reached head and shoulders above the plates. Her elevation made it impossible for Bob *not* to see what was going on. There was a tacit agreement between us that so long as he didn't actually observe any animals getting their handouts at the table, he would ignore their presence.

For Sundari's benefit, the cats demonstrated a few simple rules of their only vocation, all designed to avoid Bob's attention: first and foremost, stay away from saahib. Next, don't lie on the sideboards; long-range begging doesn't pay big dividends. Be sure to position yourself so food can be passed down without bending; saahib gets upset when kids disappear under the table. Always be prompt; be under the table before saahib arrives so he doesn't see you come in. Don't pressure guests too much; they begin to look uncomfortable, then saahib notices. Don't trip servants; what you get won't be worth the furor. Last and most important, don't bite the hand that feeds you.

Sundari kept the letter of the law while Bob was in the house because she generally bowed to his judgment. But she found the law confining when he was away and found a way to beat the cats at their own game. One evening when Bob was on tour, I was finishing dinner alone with a book propped before me. Suddenly I was conscious of a moving shadow beside the floral centerpiece: Sundari was systematically devouring petunias and zinnias one after another with the expression of a gourmet. I am sure she thought anything on the table was there for eating. Obviously, she enjoyed the flowers, because after that day she ate my flower arrangements at every chance. I'm afraid I laughed at her that first evening—a large mistake, since any caper that got a laugh was good for frequent repeats.

Up to then Sundari had not been forcibly made to do anything against her will; she had been cajoled and bribed and teased into behaving. Still I knew this trick wouldn't

55

go well with Bob. He had found occasion to criticize Sundari's behavior before. The time had come when Sundari must understand her limits, but for a brief period she maintained a bumbling decorum in the dining room that precluded any correction.

A few nights after Bob's return, our menu called for spaghetti. As usual, the advance party of beggars stood watch under the table before the dinner gong sounded. First came the family, then the salad, then spaghetti. On schedule, the feline melodrama began. Mealtimes were always a trial to Sundari because she had to share our attention with her four-legged peers; this evening she decided the time had come to retrieve her starring role. Abandoning caution, she crawled onto the back of Bob's chair. The youngsters and I were too startled to speak. But nothing happened. To this day I don't know whether or not Bob knew she was perched behind him and was simply keeping the peace. In any case, he was engrossed with the business at hand, feasting on the pasta with its mounds of scarlet sauce. His elbows were spread out to rest on the arms of his chair when Sundari eased herself between his arm and his body and slapped one fat paw squarely in his plate of spaghetti. Gobbets of red sauce and ascarids of spaghetti spiraled up like fireworks. I remember hearing one candle hiss as it drowned. Rod got the worst drenching because he sat to the right of his father. Sundari's body partially shielded Rob on the other side. But none went bare. The whole table dripped with gore.

The people at that table were paralyzed, forks halfway to mouths, jaws slack, frozen in suppressed, hilarious horror. We didn't dare look at one another. Murli was rooted to a spot midway between Rod and Jan, his tray of garlic bread tilted crazily. Sundari stood like a statue, one paw still planted in the master's plate and the other daintily poised in the air like a little finger over a teacup; she was waiting for her applause.

Bob—with nerves of steel and Sundari's body still neatly tucked under his arm—didn't move a muscle. Ruby sauce dripped from one eyebrow, but he didn't shout. He didn't even look surprised. He just suggested through clenched teeth, "Remove your damn Cat from my dinner!"

56

It took some moments for me to get my legs under me, but then I moved fast—racing the laughter that was stuck in my throat. Snagging the Cat, I dashed out of the room, reached the hall, and stuffed a fist into my mouth to stifle the sound of my laughter. While I quietly quaked, Sundari washed her face and paws. The poor kids had to sit with straight faces at the table while Murli mopped at Bob, replaced his plate, and served him more spaghetti. In a few minutes, they straggled out, limp from the agony of withholding their glee. It only needed two of us to look at each other for the laughter to explode. We howled, we choked, we rolled on the floor.

But not Bob. When he emerged from the dining room, he was still mopping sauce and he wore a spaghetti ribbon behind one ear. We broke into fresh spasms of hysteria. He ignored the laughter. Finally, when I regained my equilibrium, he made his announcement: "From now on, that leopard is banned from the dining room during mealtime."

I couldn't blame Bob. But no one had ever before said no to Sundari. She was only a cub, and she'd been playing.

I hoped that Bob would relent. But the next night his first act at dinner was to peer under the table. "Out," he said. "Take that Cat out!" Sundari was duly evicted.

She looked heartbroken as she sat in the doorway "ulping" at me. But she understood when I said "Bus" that she had to stay where she was.

The lesson, of course, was a good one for my spoiled Pretty One—and a lesson overdue. If I were starting over again with my leopard baby, I would protect Sundari far less and demand far more. At least, I would *try*. It was hard to say no to her heartbroken *ulp*.

Sundari, though, showed considerable bounce. Within two days, she had found a way to beg more food than ever. In the kitchen, she dealt directly with the cook, and Hari was easily harassed. She got the best tidbits even before the family saw them. And she didn't have to share her goodies with her Persian peers.

5

BY THE first week in September, when Sundari was three months old, she seemed becalmed in an awkward age. Huge ears dwarfed her face, and she plodded the floors flat-footed on enormous paws. Her ravaged baby pelt was just beginning to be replaced by adult fur. Her growing body was pear shaped. Altogether, she was a far cry from the embodiment of lithe grace and svelte elegance one associates with leopards. I was almost ashamed to show her to callers. Visitors, I feared, might see only her rough exterior and fail to notice what lay beneath the shabby covering. The cub's scraggly looks seemed a reflection on my maternal ability. That she was large and healthy and happy was certainly important, but it would have been more to the point had she looked it!

For all her poor physique she had an engaging minx face. And about that time we made the startling discovery that leopards have chins. There is a fleshy protuberance just below the lower lip, and though it has no bone or cartilage, it still gives the appearance of a proper chin. When jutted forward, it shows determination, even stubbornness; and in repose it lends depth to the face. The rest of her features were changing too. Her nose was broadening, and her eyes had changed from inky blue to a moss green so soft that she looked more placid than our Persians.

One of Sundari's favorite tricks was to leap from chair backs, bookshelves—wherever she happened to be roosting— onto the shoulders of passersby. She didn't use her claws to hang on so the ambush was dangerous only to herself. Unless we were prepared to catch her she took headers to the floor that would have stunned a less sturdy animal. Old wives may insist that cats always land on their feet, but their rule doesn't cover baby leopards. Sundari's leaps gave us some surprises and startled a few guests, but the only real beneficiary from this roughhouse was our tailor. A small dapper man, Kooldip stayed terrified—but grateful. Fangs and talons did catch in our clothing, so he was constantly repairing our dresses and jackets. All of us suffered a few surface scratches, only because we had our fists and arms in her mouth so much, but Rod's bitterest complaint against Sundari was, "Here I've spent months with a leopard and I haven't a scar to show for it."

Either our hides were especially tough or Sundari was more careful with us than with our belongings. Our first inkling of her great intelligence came when we watched her clear the decks for action. Her sturdy frame gave her the ability to jump, and her fertile brain the audacity to recon- noiter landing areas. As though planning a campaign, she carefully wiped all tables clear of ash trays, knickknacks, papers, books, and magazines before taking off. That way her gliding landings were unimpeded by obstructions. Our house seemed to have been decorated by a whirlwind.

When Sundari tired of flying, she stopped to munch the heaps of debris on the floor, swallowing anything from candles to carbon paper. Upright table lamps annoyed the Cat, so she went after their light bulbs, cords, and shades. She de- voured and digested all kinds of house plants. Murli became

Rob and Sundari manufacture work for the tailor. Sundari is three and a half months old. Davis

Handles are for opening doors when you're seventeen months old.
Charlotte Bush

adept with needle and thread because he had so much practice repairing damage. We were finally forced to lock—not merely shut—bed pillows inside a closet during the day. For some reason, perhaps because they ticked, she quite systematically disrupted the insides of every clock in the house.

"Is Murli too busy to wind clocks anymore?" Bob complained. And I, coward that I am, said nothing at all—and hoped Bob wouldn't directly accost Murli. But I couldn't hide Bob's gnawed hiking boots from him; Sundari had excavated a boot from the back of his closet to chew off the top of the tongue. Rod left his boots out, so he had less complaint. And I caught the culprit with my boots before they were more than pockmarked.

Sundari developed an aversion to sleeping on the floor and looked longingly at the tops of almirahs. But because she couldn't jump six feet straight up, she had to settle for berths on desks and dressers. She reached refrigerator tops—much to Hari's consternation—via the kitchen cabinets. In addition to her other talents, the cub learned early how to push open unlatched doors. She also knew the handles were there to open those doors latched by mistake. We wondered how long it would take her to open doors once she could reach the handles. We needn't have; she had figured out the mechanics by the time her paws reached that high. It took only a little practice to determine whether she had to push or pull back on the door as she released the latch. She knew that keys locked closet doors and she patted them fondly. I dreaded the day she might learn the secret of twisting those keys. What if she locked herself in a room? How would I ever explain to a maintenance crew that my leopard had locked herself in? And worse yet, how would I ever persuade them to get her out? But my worries were needless: like most children, she didn't close doors once she opened them.

Actually, her ability to open doors saved us many trips up and down steps because she kept the barsati door open. The screen door was no barrier to Nuyan and Baby Cat. The only one needing help had been Panch, and since he was

*Sundari, at three and a half months, gardening from the bottom
up.* Davis

always with Sundari he had no problem. The Lhasa Apso had passed through the doorway under the leopard's belly.

We encouraged Sundari to visit the barsati to use the pile of potting soil. She much preferred earth to the noisy papers or the sandbox. Besides, the box was rapidly becoming too small except in dire emergencies. As soon as she had ready access to the mound of sandy loam, toilet training was an accomplished fact. We had no more accidents in the house. Unlike domestic cats, Sundari did not dig a hole in which to defecate; but she scrupulously covered bowel movements. Urine she did not cover—perhaps because large cats demarcate their territory with drops of urine on trees and shrubs.

The barsati gave Sundari a new field for her curiosity. She checked out the undersides of water tanks and the back sides of gas cylinders. From the parapets she could watch the passing scene on the street below. And a promenade along the parapets made her feel quite daring; bravely she paddled through the scrub jungle Bob had trained to overhang the wall. But our joy over Sundari's successful introduction to the dirt pile was balanced by the discovery that she was an avid gardener. Bob had planted jasmine and pigeon peas in large tubs and interspersed them with smaller pots of sunflowers, petunias, balsams, and zinnias. Years earlier, he had assured me, "You can't have both a garden and a goat." At that time he'd had no experience with leopards and gardens.

Sundari's ideas on pruning and potting differed chaotically from ours. She tested annuals for scent by devouring them, and from the faces she made each had a distinctive flavor. She advised Bob about replanting by breaking the current pots. After Christmas, when the potted Christmas tree was moved upstairs to the roof, she practiced trapeze artistry among its browning needles—until it looked like a shrunken telephone pole. Then she graduated to jasmine bushes.

It didn't take long to learn that jasmine are too brittle to support acrobats heavier than ants or aphids. Bob was at first amused, then a bit testy over Sundari's inept pruning. To avert his becoming vehement, I thought it wise to remove the evidence before he got home from the office. With that

Sundari, at sixteen months, tested annuals for scent by devouring them. One of the author's favorite photographs. Davis

>

Our Christmas tree suffered from the double threat of leopard climber and mali drought. Davis

in mind I made an inspection tour of the barsati each afternoon just before five o'clock. All broken greenery I tossed over the side. That ruse worked for a week. Then Bob came home earlier than usual and alighted from the car just in time for a jasmine branch to crown his brow. For some reason he took the attitude that my actions made me an accomplice in Sundari's depredations.

The roof garden was a grand place for ambushes because the leopard's coat blended so well with any background. Sundari knew instinctively how to utilize the available cover to fullest advantage. It amazed us that a black and tan animal of Sundari's size could vanish in a tiny green bush, or against blue lawn furniture, or reclining on red bricks. Rudyard Kipling, in *The Jungle Book,* describes the leopard's ability to make itself invisible against any background, and Sundari was Kipling's living proof. When we called her from the door, she would hide in plain sight, feigning deafness until we came to find her. Then as we hunkered down to search, perhaps in a pansy clump, we were felled by Sundari descending with the force of a blockbuster. Nothing else I know can flatten one out quite like a leopard launched from six feet away!

When Sundari wasn't using our trees, the birds were. So she became an ardent bird watcher. She sat as still as she could for five minutes—her upper limit of inactivity— gazing at twittering sparrows and minute iridescent sunbirds as they flashed in and out of blossoms like black opals. She was curious but showed no inclination to catch them, and she seemed entranced by their song and flight. She listened with cocked head to warbling bulbuls: saucy little gray and black crested birds with scarlet head- and tail-lights. The cub's ears flickered delicately on soprano notes, and at deeper tones, her eyelids drooped dreamily. Her presence on the roof actually provided the songsters a measure of protection because predatory hawks were deathly afraid of her. One afternoon the leopard sat still as a sphinx in a patch of shade watching little birds flit among the leaves. Suddenly a hawk, seemingly from nowhere, plummeted toward his quarry. But in mid-plunge he caught a glimpse of the cub. Just as suddenly he banked, veered, and pulled out of his dive, screaming his rage as he climbed back to the clouds. Sundari, blinking at the sun, seemed to grin.

Indian crows, working in flocks, teased her unmercifully, swooping at her with flapping wings and raucous squawks— but they kept well out of swiping claw range. Single birds didn't bother her, but they called their relatives to join the fun. Groups of a dozen or more ganged up on the poor leopard, raising such a cry that she sometimes refused to go outside without first standing in the shadows of the doorway for several minutes to case the treetops and adjacent roofs. If she caught sight of those big black and gray birds, the tip of her tail would twitch disgustedly and one side of her quivering upper lip would show a bit of ivory. She would gurgle throaty snarls of annoyance. This was the only sort of behavior that always brought my disapprobation. It seemed to me that slithering away from cowardly birds was most unleopardlike. Retreat only encouraged the crows in their vicious sport. But Murli was more sympathetic. One afternoon I caught him standing amid potted plants, briskly flapping a tea towel heavenward and muttering dark Hindu imprecations, while Sundari waited inside for her Raleigh to clear the way.

Sundari's housetop adventures reaped unexpected benefits. From the time she was a terrier size, our neighbors watched her perambulations on the barsati walls, and thus they became accustomed to her presence from a safe distance. They accepted her as a completely natural pet for us if not for themselves. They saw the children playing with her, and they couldn't fail to note that the cub returned their affection. It became our pleasant morning ritual to wave to the Singhs, Chopras, Duttas, and Annands. Adults shouted kind, if somewhat anxious, inquiries after our health. They held babies high in the air to point out the leopard. Small children screamed, "Ta ta, Ta, ta!" and hopped on toothpick legs to attract our attention. Neighbors who lived farther afield began smiling at us on the street, and some stopped to ask questions. What was Sundari's age? What did she eat? Where did she sleep? And most particularly, weren't we afraid of her? We gladly answered their questions, knowing every answer decreased the chances that someone would object. Sundari herself more effectively bridged a culture gap than all the words in a dictionary. Conversation convinced the neighbors in our adopted community that we were very much like them. Maybe our pet was not one they would have chosen, but that wasn't important. They were genuinely pleased to have a part, however small, in the integration of a leopard into human society.

Around our apartment, Murli's ideas on leopard-rearing most nearly coincided with mine: we agreed Sundari could do no wrong. We felt she should not be fettered by tedious rules, and that those who disagreed with us lacked proper perspective. We also shared a great ignorance about leopards, but at least Murli could excuse his failing on the grounds that he had never heard of such a beast till she came to live with us. Occasionally I fell by the wayside, as in the matter of crows, and once in a while I tried to head Sundari into the paths of righteousness. But so far as I know, Murli never faltered behind her lead. When I showed a lack of understanding, Murli's scowl and manner suggested that I didn't deserve to own a leopard.

One morning Sundari tried to steal the bacon as it was frying in the skillet. She burned her thieving paws, and I said, "Serves her right!" She would get no comfort from me. Not Murli. He seemed distracted for a few minutes, then frowned. "I feed," he said. "Memsaahib make holiday."

Behind his words was an implication. Sundari, if left to his care, wouldn't have to singe her paws to get bacon. But the suggestion had merit. Thereafter, Murli happily slopped together egg yolk, pabulum cereal, and boiled buffalo while Sundari stood at his side. Her paws rested on the counter edge, and she sagely nodded her head as he explained the intricacies of diet and the virtues of patience.

Still, I reserved the right to hand-feed Sundari part of every meal. For good reason. She must never object to being handled while eating. We had too many people in our house— strangers as well as residents—to allow her any latitude in the matter. She must never question that the giver of food

69

could also take the meal away at any time. More than once impaled bones had to be pried from her molars, and had she not found it perfectly normal to have my fingers in her mouth, I would lack a few today. Cats are by nature dainty eaters, and Sundari, raised in our arms, found it natural to receive food from our hands. Her training in this respect was simply to continue her accustomed feeding pattern.

The whole household enjoyed feeding Sundari, and her tastes developed in a way no leopard's should. Perhaps Hari fed the Cat out of self-interest, but the children shared food with her because it wouldn't have occurred to them not to. Rob's passion for raw coconut could account for Sundari's. I introduced her to pepperoni. But of all her delicatessen delights, she most enjoyed cheeses—cheeses of all ages, flavors, and consistencies. She also relished salads with Thousand Island or French dressing.

Jan shared her Popsicles with Nuyan on one side and Sundari on the other. Shares were equal, and both cats politely waited for the stick to be passed their way. Sundari, however, usually got the leopard's share because she had the broadest tongue; and once in a while she forgot herself and closed her mouth on the stick instead of giving it a ladylike lick. When that happened, her two companions had no recourse; the whole ice fitted neatly into a leopard mouth—pulling on the stick only left the contents right where Sundari intended them to be. Of course, the practice was unsanitary. But everyone stayed healthy, and the trust engendered in all three could hardly have been duplicated in any other way. Guests seemed more at ease after watching Sundari take food from our fingers. And those callers courageous enough to offer her tidbits of cheese themselves left us with a far higher estimate of their own bravery.

In the autumn when school reopened, Sundari's busy day began early. After thoroughly rasping Bob and me with her morning kisses, she proceeded to the barsati bedroom to rouse the boys. Rob had no school bus to meet and would have cheerfully postponed the pleasure of her attention; he accepted her visit with as little animation as she would permit. Following a quick stop at the dirt pile, she trotted downstairs to check on the girls. Kris was usually awake but feigned sleep so she wouldn't disappoint the Cat. For Jan, the slugabed, Sundari was a highly effective wake-up service. No one can sleep with a leopard flopping and moaning all over her.

Missions to the children accomplished, she greeted Hari and Murli in the kitchen. There she sneaked a bite of breakfast before stationing herself in the dining room. The location was safe, she knew, because Bob only has a cup of coffee, brought to the bedroom, in the morning. Thus her exhausting job was done. With children off to school, Sundari went back to bed—this time with Rob—to catch a catnap until he would get up and play with her.

With Panch gone, Rob became her favorite playmate. He hadn't much else to do, and he was strong enough to indulge in free-for-all wrestling. I declined those games on the grounds she always won. No matter where she was, she could hear his softly whispered *"psst psst,"* and knew it signaled *tag.* Skidding and sliding over tables, scattering cats and servants, overturning chairs, they galloped through the flat punctuating their progress with resounding clangs and depressing crashes. Rob complained, "She doesn't play fair, Mom. I'm not allowed to jump onto furniture, and she never gets blamed for anything." Anything meant everything. Rob insisted it wasn't his fault when his bed frame broke in half. I maintained it was because if he hadn't been on top of the almirah she wouldn't have been thrashing around on the bed trying to get him. We quietly shored up the sagging bed springs with bricks and didn't ask his father's opinion.

The whole family—well, all but Bob—played hide-and-seek with the leopard. One of us would call, "I'm gonna get YOU!" and Sundari would race to hide so she wouldn't be It. She had several favorite hiding places and none of the inhibitions that prevented her playmates from climbing into Bob's jasmine bushes or Ram Prashad's washing machine. To this day I don't know how a black-and-gold animal can vanish against a pink shower curtain. She not only availed herself of camouflage, but she also cheated without remorse. When

Kris pretends to be asleep so Sundari, sixteen months old, can wake her up. Charlotte Bush

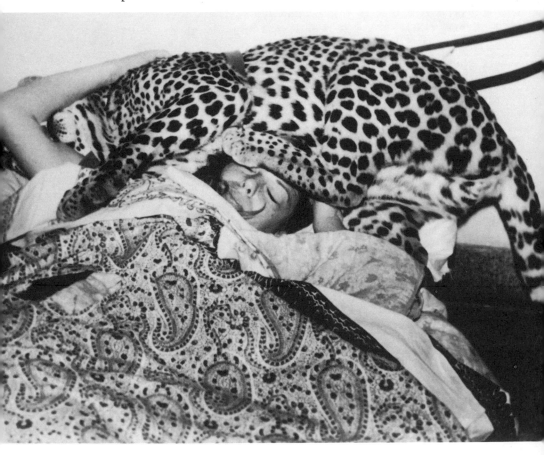

she was It, she refused to close her eyes while counting. We had only two advantages over her. She thought that as long as we couldn't see her eyes, she was hidden from view. It was all we could do to suppress laughter when we saw two ears gliding along a table edge as though floating on air. Our other advantage was to wait until she had stalked us almost to our hiding place, then leap out flapping our arms and hollering, "BOOO!" It must be terribly disconcerting to a leopard to have a silent stalk ruined when the quarry suddenly turns aggressive; but Sundari, after a second's glassy-eyed stalemate, would pirouette high in the air, land running, and hit home base before we could get a start.

Next to playing tag and hide-and-seek, she liked to help the servants at their household chores. She was particularly adept at dusting; she carefully wiped the tables clear of objets d'art before grasping a corner of Murli's dustcloth in her teeth. Together they attacked the furniture like a pair of lumberjacks with a crosscut saw.

When Murli squatted on the breakfast room floor to polish brass, she sneaked up behind to jump on his shoulders. As the jug of polish danced on the floor, the contents splattered all objects needing polish. That way, the children reasoned, Murli rarely had to expend energy tilting the bottle. Sundari proved herself invaluable to the bearer in the dining room when he changed the table cloth. After he spread it over the table, Murli relied on Sundari to equalize the overhang on all sides. If sometimes his assistant waited to align hems till after the table was set for supper, her overexuberance wasn't Murli's fault. Without comment he harvested the sugar, salt, and pepper strewn on the floor. Man and beast made a game of cleaning up the bedrooms; they invented a form of two-man soccer with Sundari playing goalie and defending the closet against shoes, hats, and belts that Murli lobbed in her direction.

"Those two have totaled my room," Jan complained. But in reality, Sundari performed a very useful service: the youngsters learned to put away their possessions.

Sundari hit her stride cleaning bathrooms. As a small

cub, she showed Murli the dust that had accumulated behind commodes by parading through it and tracking it across his freshly mopped floors. By the time she was four months old she began cleaning bathtubs. Murli crouched over the tub to sprinkle the scouring powder while Sundari leaned her torso over the side to watch. She couldn't turn the faucet knob for rinse water, but when Murli did, she could indeed slap the lever switching on the shower. Not once did Murli lose his temper—or drown.

The dhobi reacted with less grace. He came three times a week to wash and iron. He seemed to feel he didn't need her to jerk clothes through the wringer. When Sundari noticed his rinse tubs, full of tepid water and newly washed clothes, she waded right in. Ram Prashad visibly shuddered. When he carried the wet things to the barsati to hang on the line, she followed. As he snappily flapped a piece before pinning it to the line, she soared over his shoulder to catch the billowing material. When he finally got the clothes hung out, the Cat continued to watch the waving pennants—and then pulled them down. When she tried to deliver poor Ram Prashad's fresh ironing to its owners, he became distraught.

"Memsaahib, it is no good," the dhobi told me. "You must be tying Sundari with ropes." We compromised by shutting Ram Prashad himself in the godown with his iron and board and laundry.

Even with such strenuous activities, Sundari found time to meet each member of the household at the door. Instinctive caution prevented her from going beyond the first stair landing, but she waited there each day for Hari to return from the bazaar. She knew he would have vegetables for her to carry to the kitchen—or a bone to divert her attention. Whether or not the rest of us heard him come in, we could always tell when Hari had been to market: he crawled through the apartment on all fours retrieving bruised vegetables and fruit.

On hot afternoons Sundari deployed herself across a charpoy, to nap in the deep aquamarine shade of the front porch. It was always curious to me—on my own insomniacal days—to watch the climate work like an anesthetic. By one o'clock, parakeets had stopped arguing with chipmunks over possession of the trees, and the morning breeze had soughed away. Men in the streets dropped where they stood as though poleaxed, dhotis flung over their heads to ward off evil spirits as they slept. Across the street under the neem tree, the tiny ancient biirdii-wallah dozed; street urchins took advantage of his dreams to snitch free cigarettes. The soggy enervating temperature soared and for two hours India simply ceased to function. In winter, north Indians curse the sun for its capricious vitality, in summer they pray for deliverance, and in monsoon they gratefully drink in its watery rays. But wet or dry, shivering or sweating, India sleeps from one till three.

Then we watched India waken. Sleeping men stirred on their brick pallets; yawning, they gathered themselves to finish the day. Birds uttered tentative arguments, cumulus clouds began their assault on the sun, and the biirdii-wallah—salvaging his wares and scolding the street thieves—awakened Sundari.

She stretched, refreshed, and languidly eased off the cot to get a drink of water. Then she returned to watch the unfolding drama and to listen for a special sound. Suddenly her head tipped sideways, whiskers dancing in anticipation and great green eyes wide with pleasure. She wheeled and flashed toward the stairs. Her school bus was coming. The bus, still out of sight, was just turning into Nizam-ud-Din East, but she heard it and knew her people were aboard. Though at least a score of other buses passed our door, Sundari never missed.

"Of course," we speculated, "she knows the time." But so many other buses were plying the same route at the same time that it couldn't have been the whole answer. Somehow she knew. She waited on the lower landing with a smiling face and a body dancing while her tail swayed like a charmed snake. Each day was the same; she missed her playmates and wanted them to know it.

She met Bob more sedately in the hall, aware that he frowned on unseemly displays. Often, too, Bob brought home a guest—necessitating retreat for the Cat until the newcomer had been thoroughly surveyed. If all seemed safe, she joined Bob on the couch while he sipped his sundowner. In his presence she was far more subdued than at other times, for she correctly interpreted his serious demeanor as a desire for peace. And while the teen-agers paraded before their father their complaints—an interminable exhibition of ripped shirts, gnawed shoes, and tattered schoolbooks, Sundari self-consciously nibbled her nail or toyed with the tip of her tail.

Sundari accepted the children's friends as her own. Perhaps one reason was that youngsters treated her like any other pet, neither deferring to her nor ignoring her. They simply patted her head and continued their business of eating, gossiping, and dancing. Though their music might sound like chalk on a blackboard, it didn't bother Sundari. She grew up to think shuffling feet and grinding music were natural.

Indians, with the exception of our three servants, were a different story. The Cat's early mistrust turned to dislike, and there seemed to be no remedy for it. The problem developed almost immediately. Whenever Indians visited us, Sundari wanted nothing to do with them. I tried to find the reason, and the only logical answer I could find was attitude and color. I cannot believe, as some authorities assert, that a leopard's distrust could arise from an odor exuded by those who feared her. Sundari's sense of smell wasn't that acute. But her instinct about human attitudes was unerring. And eventually, I think, she came to associate those unfriendly attitudes with darker skin color.

Most westerners approached Sundari with admiration for her species as well as respect for her position in our lives. If they also questioned our sanity, they didn't blame the Cat. Indians, almost invariably, looked askance not only at us but at her. All too often their attitude toward Sundari was colored by Hindu attitudes toward a lower order. And perhaps a bit of social resentment. That the members of an alien society chose to indulge their far-out whim could only be regarded by some as ostentatious. I could appreciate that feeling. A leopard in a city apartment is indeed a way-out whim. They neither

76

understood nor accepted Sundari's presence as a member of our household. Yet had we caged her as a wild beast, they could have accepted her as a curiosity. Without bars between a predator cat and themselves, their superiority dwindled, the barrier of station and caste blurred. On an equal footing they became defensive. They rejected Sundari's intelligence as a challenge to their own. Sundari could sense their resentment. The only persons who ever mistreated her or actively disdained her were Indian. And so she came to associate dark hair and skin with unpleasantness and fear.

Maintenance crews made no effort to hide their fear. They actively avoided contact with Sundari, and since her desire matched theirs, there was no danger of a meeting. When repairmen worked in the apartment, the Cat wrapped herself around one of us for protection. One October evening two plumbers came on an emergency call while we were at dinner. Sundari, then in the kitchen, retreated to the refrigerator top with Hari to stand guard for her. The men went up to the barsati to make their repairs, and after dinner the three older children and I began a game of bridge. Sundari crawled out of hiding to sit beside me instead of going to bed. Involved in our game, we forgot that the workmen were still in the house until a timid voice called from the hall, "Memsaahib? Please, we want to go now."

There in the doorway stood the plumber. He looked as though instead of fixing a leaky faucet he had just dammed the River Styx.

"Well, fine," I said. "Do you want me to sign your work order?" I wondered why it had taken three hours to do a fifteen-minute job.

"Your bil-un-cheetah is holding my peon on the barsati," the plumber was stuttering in his terror.

"But that's not possible! Sundari is here with me. Look, see for yourself!"

He wouldn't look at the spot I pointed out, but rolled his eyes heavenward and shook his head.

"N-no. The cheetah w-won't let my p-peon go."

I was truly puzzled. "I don't know what you think is after your peon, but it's not Sundari. She's here. But come along, we'll see what's going on!"

We climbed the steps, the apologetic plumber at my heels. Tears would have been more appropriate than laughter for the forlorn scene that greeted us. A little brown man squatted— teetering—on the parapet; his fingers convulsively clutched a drainpipe. His eyes rolled in abject fear. How long he had been there is anybody's guess. But the animal holding him prisoner—by staring up at the man—was none other than our little red Persian. I scooped Baby Cat into my arms while the plumber rescued his helper, and then I tried to explain to them the difference between a leopard and a Persian cat. It was all of a piece to them.

In India logic frequently proved a weak reed. Hari, for example, came to me one morning with an urgent announcement.

"In the village," he said, "the roof has fallen upon my daughter-in-law's head."

I was genuinely alarmed, and promptly gave Hari three days' leave. Not until later did I learn that falling roofs are second in popularity only to mothers' deathbeds as pretexts for the vacations of cooks.

Two weeks later we received a note from Hari. In careful script, he told us, "I cannot leave." Hari gave us no firm details; presumably he was holding up the roof.

We had no choice but to begin interviewing other cooks. The news that we were cookless rocketed across Delhi. Within two hours after we'd received Hari's note, I had answered the door no less than fifteen times to job applicants. Most were snaggle-toothed old men, unkempt, and rusty-lipped from chewing betel. Not one of them was clean enough to set foot in a kitchen. Some looked diseased. Others resembled dacoits. Yet each claimed miraculous prowess with foods. All of them —beggars, lepers, thieves—backed up their preposterous claims with grubby dog-eared chits of ancient vintage and doubtful authenticity. The clanging doorbell kept Sundari from her usual rounds; she confined herself to our bedroom and preened herself before the mirror. I rather hoped she would appear to frighten away the fainthearted in that ragged army of unemployed, and unemployable, cooks. But she kept herself meekly out of sight, so the locustlike plague of applicants continued.

Shortly after Sundari had joined our family I had nailed a brass plate to our front door. It said, *"Beware of the leopard"* in bold Hindi and English. I should have known better: those the message was supposed to scare couldn't read either script. Still, as I plodded down the steps for perhaps the thirtieth time, I thought, if the Cat won't help me, maybe that brass plate will. I opened the door on an obese, stubble-chinned old man; one eye was pinched shut in an owlish, confidential wink. He was villainously dirty and, if one of the aromas emanating from his person was an indication, a trifle drunk. Without any greeting I asked, "Can you read?"

He wagged his head and answered, "Yes, yes."

"Good! What does this sign say?"

Squinting his good eye in piratical fashion, he deciphered the legend. In a drinking man's whisper he laughed, "Ha, ha, Madam! That's a good sign. That will keep beggars and thieves away."

"Well," I said, "It isn't meant to scare. Our leopard is a ferocious man-eater. Our last cook left because"—I paused to think. Lies for the simpleminded have to be bad enough for them to believe—"because, uh, she ate his left arm off."

But while I was blackening her reputation, the man-eater of the house poked an angelic face around the corner of the balustrade to see what was keeping me so long. She sat down and benignly placed her forepaws on the floor and her rear end on the first step to watch. She even bobbed her head as if in confirmation of the awful absurdities rolling off my tongue. The patent untruthfulness of the words struck the poor man as entirely plausible. Fortunately he didn't see Sundari at all.

Licking dry lips with a cottony tongue, he began a hasty retreat with the agility of one accustomed to fast getaways. Turning on my peaceful pet, I snipped at her, "You might have ruined the whole thing! You could at least *act* like a man-eater once in a while!"

Later, Rod suggested a better recovery in case Sundari ever made similar stage entrances—"This one's not so bad, but you ought to see her mother!"

Since the last cook wasn't around to contest the story, news of his tragedy swept the Delhi underworld with great dispatch. Few souls dared face Nizam-ud-Din's fabled man-eater! Applications dropped off. Then, two days later, a Muslim with the improbable cognomen of Fuzzle, more courageous than most, appeared on our doorstep. His references, little short of marvelous, proclaimed him a paragon of virtue in a profession noted for side benefits and kickbacks. Past employers even called him an excellent cook. None of his references postdated Partition, but in a clear voice he said, "No, Madam, I do not fear leopards."

I hired him on the basis of his bravado. And in succeeding days, though Sundari did her best to unhinge his armor of confidence, he proved a match for the darling of the house.

Sundari liked Fuzzle for the simple reason that he didn't dislike her. He was of the live-and-let-live school—though his sentiments were probably engendered by American wage incentive. But whatever the reason, they got along, and that's what mattered with us.

Fuzzle's appearance on the domestic scene brought new skirmishes of psychological warfare for Sundari. Fuzzle, in fact, helped the leopard hone her sense of humor to a degree we hadn't thought possible. She put great effort into devising practical jokes to play on the cook; but though he often stumbled, Fuzzle rarely lost his poise. At any hour of the day we might hear his voice in an ascending scale, "Aah, AAh, AAH!" And Sundari would surge from the kitchen showing every sign of a foiled leopard. She tried sitting atop the refrigerator and as he passed beneath her she would pat his balding pate. When that trick failed to elicit more than a grunt, she tried sticking her head inside when he opened the refrigerator door.

"I do not mind her head in the icebox, Madam," said Fuzzle, "but I fear I shall catch it when the door is closed."

80

"Don't worry," I replied, "her head and all her teeth will still be inside."

Initial failure didn't deflect Sundari from her purpose. She began crossing the kitchen from the top of one refrigerator to the other—using Fuzzle's head as a stepping stone. Steel nerves corseted his spine. Neither did he flinch when she scaled the heights of the cabinets and knocked down a storm of potato-chip tins and cake racks around his ears. But her persistence paid off. A simple tactic finally fractured Fuzzle's calm: she would drop into a springing crouch whenever he saw her. That blew Fuzzle's nonchalance. The instant he saw her begin to sag, his "AAHs" hit a fearful pitch.

But much as she enjoyed teasing Fuzzle, Sundari had the sense to desist as the dinner hour neared. She had no desire to disrupt the kitchen at that hour of the day. So she moved her pranks toward the rest of us. She thoroughly enjoyed seeing parcels, schoolbooks, or cats spilling from our arms. She found two ways to bring about such a display. She could hide behind a door and leap out at the right moment. But ambushes didn't always work. Sometimes she wasn't sufficiently careful to secrete a patch of tail or pink-gray nose.

The second tactic took more time to set the stage. First, she had to decide on a suitable doorway—usually one of the two hall doors leading to the front and back of the apartment. A steady flow of pedestrian traffic passed through those portals. Perhaps one quarter of those pedestrians sprawled flat on their faces. None of us at first attributed our breakneck headers to any deliberate malice—until we caught onto a pattern.

To accomplish this one, Sundari lay down near the doorway and composed her face into a vacant expression. Her face should have been the warning; it was never blank except when contemplating or denying sin. As someone walked by, she made one swift pass, jabbing out an arm stiff as a fence post between the legs of the passerby. Like a shot from a cannon, she felled the best of us. From the depths of personal experience, I know it takes some minutes to determine where you are and how you got there. You might notice a smiling, slumbering leopard in the vicinity, but for some time you're too disoriented to link cause and effect. Later, after you shout an accusing, "SOON-da-ree!" you find a leopard swarming all over you with kisses to restore the peace.

With fraudulent innocence she spared Bob. Among the rest of us there were some who churlishly wished she would spring that trap on Bob once—just once was all we asked. She'd be a long time doing it again! On Saturdays and Sundays she pattered along beside him in a deplorably benign pose, lulling him into a false sense of camaraderie. She helped him plant seedlings by jamming her paw into the pot so it wouldn't blow away, and she dragged his hose inside where the flowing water didn't puddle around his bare feet. During heat-soaked siesta hours, while he slept under fan and air-conditioner, she snuggled close to his perspiring form to protect him from catching cold in the chill breezes. Bob thought that her exemplary weekend behavior revealed a change of heart. But Sundari was operating on the theory that what Bob didn't personally observe she wouldn't get blamed for. She so warped his thought processes that he once said, "Sundari, you're a sorely maligned youngster. You wouldn't get into so much trouble if the others didn't encourage you."

But one Sunday he got an inkling of the truth. The leopard in his castle hadn't changed her spots at all.

By some unhappy chance, maintenance crews reserved Sunday mornings for routine calls to our apartment, so that each Sunday we picked our way through painters and plumbers. Finally it dawned on us that these workmen had simply been thrown out of other houses on the day of rest. On the morning of that revelation, a crew of workmen had materialized on the upper landing without even knocking. Sundari, cut off from her bedroom hideaway, cowered behind Bob's legs while he faced the crew in exasperation. "Do you only come here because you can't work elsewhere on Sundays?"

"Yes, yes," they agreed in singsong unison.

"Okay!" said Bob, "Leopard sick 'em! Eat 'em up! Eat 'em up!"

She tried, but Sundari wasn't the stuff heroines are made of. Her face puckered in an effort to assume the angry mien

82

Bob decided that Sundari was a much maligned four-month-old youngster. Davis

of carnivorous cats; she only succeeded in looking like a baby leopard making faces and peeking between her saahib's knees. Bob tried to shove her forward with one foot, but she wasn't having any part of that. She planted her paws firmly in the calf of his other leg. It didn't matter anyway. The work gang had already bolted down the steps.

Trying to disentangle himself, Bob bitterly denounced her cowardice. "Why can't you *act* like a watchdog?"

But meek as she seemed when we wanted her to be otherwise, Sundari needed some kind of discipline. She was steadily reducing the living room to a shambles. Her awkward strength was equal to that of a domestic animal three times her size; her endurance at jokes and games was discouraging. Nothing had disturbed her peace of mind. We had overprotected her; we had even forbidden flashbulb pictures of her for fear of upsetting her psyche. She was now getting too smart-alecky for her own good, and it wasn't fair to the rest of the household. Sooner or later she would bully the servants beyond good fun and it would be too late to correct her.

She already knew when I yipped, "What are you DOING?" that she had better quit, at least until I was out of sight. But she betrayed no real regret and returned to her destructive games as soon as my back was turned.

But how does one start disciplining a leopard? She learned so easily that it wasn't unfair to ask her to remember a few rules of our choosing. The familiar spankings with a folded paper didn't seem logical; how could she be paddled with them one minute and expected to use them the next? Shaking a fly swatter under her nose didn't work at all; she ate the lacy part and broke the handle in four pieces.

If remanded to our bedroom, she treated the excursion as one big joke—on me. She amused herself playing farmerette: she sowed the rug with bobby pins, fertilized them with liquid makeup, and filled the wastebasket water trough with perfume, throwing the bottle in for good measure. When rural pastimes paled, she barked for us to get her out—and the muffled tone of her voice made me think she was suffocating. She wasn't—her mouth was clogged with great chunks of bedding. After two of her disciplinary stretches in that room, our belongings couldn't have served a poorhouse.

We had to find another way to train her; but had my life depended on it, I couldn't have disciplined her harshly. I was overprotective and underfirm and I knew it. Why? Because she was a leopard, or because she was so intelligent? Probably it was a mixture of both. Every time she patted my face with a chamois-soft paw, or played tag with my son, or ate ice cream with my daughter, or ran to meet my husband, she gave fresh evidence that she was a fully integrated member of the family. That Sundari, a great cat, should accept my way as hers filled me with awe. I could fold my arms around her spotted furry body and bury my nose in that silken neck and her eyes lighted with a warmth that melted my heart.

A leopard is an animal eminently self-sufficient, yet here was Sundari putting all her trust in fallible mankind. Such trust is a gift rarely given, and I only hoped we'd be worthy of that trust.

6

WHILE SUNDARI was still a toddling cub, Mrs. Davis of the Washington Zoo sent me an especially helpful bit of information: "Few leopards have been raised as pets, but I do know one in California. The owner trains animals for television, so you might write her."

And thus I got the address of Mrs. Marge Sparrow. I wrote her at once asking for suggestions, but by the time our letters had moved around the world Sundari was four months old.

"How lucky you are to have a leopard!" wrote Mrs. Sparrow. No one else had ever told us such a thing, so her letter was like a cool breath of air on a hot summer day. Mrs. Sparrow confirmed what I had already felt in my heart to be true: that steady, even discipline plus patience and love would make us Sundari's slaves for life. She expected her own leopard Shezade to become *more* rather than less affectionate at maturity. "Sundari will return what you give tenfold," said Mrs. Sparrow.

Several times later when I felt baffled and lonely with the problems of Sundari, I reread Mrs. Sparrow's first letter; each time it gave me encouragement. Mrs. Sparrow was the one person who knew what Sundari was and what she meant to us. She ended her letter with a wise summary of our adventure: "No one owns a leopard, but a fortunate few are owned by them."

I can count on the fingers of one hand those persons outside our family who have been able to accept Sundari wholeheartedly. The spectre of the fabled predator loomed too large. No one had the understanding of Mrs. Sparrow, yet friends, relatives, visitors, foes, acquaintances, and sages all gave advice—whether or not it was sought. For my own convenience, I divided all advisors into two categories: those who were experienced in handling large cats and those who were not. The former I called "authorities" and the latter I called "leopardologists." The leopardologists far outnumbered the authorities. With the exception of Mrs. Sparrow, I disagreed with or doubted all of them. Such an attitude fostered many self-doubts, though, for I often recalled the adage: "Sometimes I think the whole world is crazy but thee and me . . ."

Not one of the three real authorities with whom I consulted—one American, one European, and one Indian—could understand Sundari as a member of our family. Each was highly qualified to speak on the subject of large cats as a whole, but none of them could understand one individual animal with a complex personality and feelings. Each, in his own way, warned me that we were living dangerously. Each begged me to believe his advice. Yet I, so emotionally bound to Sundari, was unable to bring them an understanding of her relationship to us. Each one gave his advice with complete kindness. I have appreciated their concern. Probably once a month I read in a paper that a lion or tiger had mauled some person—but almost invariably the offending animal had been hauled before the public and forced into a situation where sights, sounds, and unusual movements were frightening. I realized that unforeseen events could push us into the same unpredictable situation. And yet I couldn't admit the possibility.

Among the leopardologists I soon diagnosed a strange disease—an illness I call leoparditis. The symptoms include a tendency to expound at great length on the habits, attitudes, agility, and unpredictability of leopards. The illness rarely strikes children and teen-agers. Like most diseases, it can develop into a serious case or be a very gentle affliction.

Mrs. Vijay Dar, our Hindi teacher and a native of the Kashmir Himalayas, had contracted a particularly virulent form of leoparditis. She regularly warned me of the dangers of playing with wild animals—especially leopards. At last one afternoon I was goaded into asking, "Mrs. Dar, have you ever seen a leopard?"

"Certainly," she said. "I've been to the zoo, and my father told me . . ."

"Did you ever see one wild in Kashmir?" I continued.

"Not exactly, but they were all around and they're very bad. Rocky, you just don't know . . ."

"Come on, Mrs. Dar. This afternoon you must meet Sundari. I promise she won't eat you." Behind my invitation was the hope that even if Mrs. Dar could not accept Sundari's attachment to us, at least we could make her forget some of those horror stories.

Bob, leaning back on two legs of his chair, and Suzie Stamberg, another student, smiled at the exchange. Suzie volunteered, "I'd like to see her, too. I can take you home afterward, Mrs. Dar."

"How about to a hospital?" laughed Mrs. Dar. "Will you take me there, too?" Despite her trepidation, she really wanted to see Sundari. She had cut off her own retreat, so, good sport that she was, she accepted the invitation.

Sundari heard the car as it pulled up to the house and was already on the first landing to meet me. She hadn't expected company, and when she realized that I wasn't alone it was too late to beat a retreat. Nervously, the Cat leaped into my arms for protection and for her usual greeting. The roughhouse reunion did nothing to offset Mrs. Dar's concern for my safety—and for my sanity. Carrying some twenty pounds of leopard in my arms, I carefully seated Mrs. Dar in a chair opposite the green one Sundari and I used. We had the length of the coffee table between us, for I certainly had no intention of letting Sundari play a joke on the teacher. I needn't have worried because, after a two-hour absence, Sundari found my face not to her liking. She set about washing me with a thoroughness that left my cheeks tingling and my eyebrows almost depilated. If Sundari couldn't scour the newcomers, the next best thing was Mom.

Suzie laughed, but Mrs. Dar was shocked. "Rocky! You must stop this," she said. "The leopard will hurt you!"

I tried to explain that Sundari was only trying to show how much she had missed me. I pushed Sundari's mug away from my own to talk, but the Cat had found a new audience and insisted she had missed the nose. Sundari knew we were talking about her, and she was showing off: to complete her task she slapped away my fending hands.

"How old is she?" Suzie asked.

"Four months," I said through fingers, still trying to save my nose.

"You don't think you can let her do that when she's twice that age, do you?" Mrs. Dar insisted.

"I surely do! As long as Sundari lives with us she'll be kissing me."

"Well," said Mrs. Dar, "I'll bet she won't."

It was a challenge. "I'll bet you a lunch at the Taj room of the Oberoi Hotel that on February 9 next year I'll let Sundari lick my face," I said. "She'll be eight months old that day. Is it a bet?"

"I'm witness to the contract," Suzie laughed.

"It's a deal, and I think you're crazy!" Mrs. Dar smiled. She had been such a good sport about Sundari that I felt she deserved a reprieve. I called Rob to take the Cat and keep her occupied on the barsati while we finished our coffee.

"I'll win that bet," I told Mrs. Dar, "if I lose a nose trying." Nothing could have made me admit how tender my nose felt at the moment.

"You probably will!" Mrs. Dar laughed.

Not four months, but a full year later Mrs. Dar was still direly predicting my ruin, and Sundari was still lavishing her kisses on my face. I won my wager hands down, but refused collection as unfair. I knew Sundari loved me.

Sundari was unique. Though we insisted to friends that she was not unusual, we knew she was. At four months, she had quite literally developed by leaps and bounds. Her head had caught up with the size of her body and her ears. Her fat little body was slimming to a more mature appearance, so that her huge paws and heavy legs seemed more in scale. The little thorn which had been her tail at birth now measured fifteen inches; it was also one of the most expressive features of her anatomy. Dull grayish baby fuzz had given place to silken black rosettes that curled into lopsided circles against a field of old gold on her flanks and back. Her chest had become a surrealistice ebony lace on a sheet of snowy velvet. She no longer looked like a stuffed toy but was now a miniature leopard—still awkward, but here and there we caught a glimpse of the haunting liquid grace of the adult in motion. She was prideful of her budding beauty and spent her odd moments on personal grooming. When confronted with the evidence of misdeeds she turned busily—defensively—to her beauty treatments. By turns she was gay and pensive, demanding and obedient, discerning and unheeding, destructive and gentle. But whatever her mood, she was actively demonstrative in her affection for her family.

She displayed an intelligence beyond any I had observed in other animals, keenly perceptive of moods and alert to any changes in voice, gesture, or glance. She gauged her behavior to suit the moment. Hunters have covered reams of paper describing leopard cunning, of how "one must think like the leopard" to catch one. They flatter themselves. The leopard thinks like the hunter, and the hunter deceives himself that he is smarter. Sundari's affection alone would have won our devotion, but we also fell prey to the insufferable pride of those loved by leopards. It is not pride in the animal itself. Rather, we realized that an animal of such intelligence loves by free choice. That very freedom ensnared us.

90

Sundari talked to us. Though it wasn't English, her language of pantomine needed no interpreter. The gleam of her eye, slant of whiskers, jut of chin, tilt of head, angle of ears, sweep of tail—all combined to express her opinions. She understood words in both Hindi and English, and I had great fun boasting that we had the only bilingual leopard in India. Like indulgent grandparents we enjoyed everything she did. Though she often committed transgressions, she showed such dramatic flair that it was impossible not to laugh at her. And who can discipline children while laughing?

It was the lack of discipline that Mr. Sankhala insisted must be corrected in both method and severity. We disagreed. Yet I respected his knowledge, and knew that should we ever need help, he and the zoo would do everything possible. At our invitation he visited us regularly.

My concern was always for Sundari's physical progress; I knew her mental state was good. But Mr. Sankhala worried about behavioral aspects. One afternoon in October, Sundari brought the argument to a head. Visiting us, Mr. Sankhala was seated in the chair Sundari kept reserved for herself and me. She allowed other people to occupy it, but considered them fair game for teasing if they dared. On that day, she grabbed the cushion from behind him and yanked it to the floor. Then she began a reasonable imitation of a leopard eating a pillow. Mr. Sankhala remarked, "Sundari has so much confidence in your approval that she doesn't know where to draw the line. Don't you ever punish her?"

"Not if I can avoid it," I said, "but there are some things she isn't allowed to do and she knows what they are." He dismissed my answer as I tried to disengage the pillow. Sundari kept her fangs clamped; she swatted my hands with her forepaws and dug her hind feet into the small of my back. It was a game. Had I really wanted the pillow I could have made her give it up.

"You should smack her nose, then she'd understand," our visitor advised.

I was appalled at the idea of slapping Sundari in the face. Why do such a thing when she didn't need it? Once when she had tried to make a meal of a mink stole, I had administered a healthy crack on her rear—and Sundari had known immediately that velvet-lined fur was not leopard food. But her face? Never! It just wasn't necessary.

"But she isn't afraid of people," Mr. Sankhala insisted, "and it's going to lead to trouble."

"She's very shy of people she doesn't know," I replied. "Would you really have me teach her fear?"

"Yes!" he said. "She isn't afraid of you and she should be. You have raised a completely happy and uninhibited leopard. I didn't think it could be done—but that's just the problem. She could turn on you at any moment."

"If she were in the jungle, would she turn on her mother?" I asked.

"That's not the same thing at all. You are evading the problem." Mr. Sankhala was serious in his conviction: we were not safe in the company of a nonfearing leopard. Since he had brought Sundari and me together, he felt responsible for the tragedy he now expected. Mr. Sankhala mistakenly assumed that if the Cat was unafraid, we were not. And so we could not cope with her. That was not the case. For Sundari, the only difference between our home and the jungle was that we didn't wear spots. I had watched smaller feline mothers put up with a lot of foolishness from their babies; but when the time came to stop, they didn't hesitate. Neither did I. Nor had I ever seen a kitten anything but subdued after parental reprimand; and kittens are not fearful. I didn't want Sundari afraid of me or anyone in our home; on the day she first feared us, I felt certain we *would* be in danger.

"I correspond with a lady in California who has a leopard two and a half years old," I told Mr. Sankhala. "And her leopard is still gentle."

"Then it must be very unusual," said the director. "I have dealt with leopards for years, and I know them well. The species is crafty and unpredictable."

Nonetheless I was sure we could predict. "If you annoy a wild leopard you know it will charge, don't you?" I asked. "And I know if you bother Sundari she will hide. Isn't that predicting?"

92

"But if you aren't with her, and if I annoy her, do you know her reaction?" he asked.

"Yes," I replied. "You'd never get the chance because she'd be hiding under my bed."

"All right, and if I went to your room? What then?"

"She might attack you," I admitted.

"You see! You can't say with certainty what course of action she will follow." He laughed and so did I.

"Yes, I really can," I giggled, "because you are far too smart to try—I'm certain of that. Anyway, would you walk into a leopard den in the jungle?"

"Not on purpose. But we're too far astray. The point is that Sundari is not afraid of you and she should be. You must believe me."

Mr. Sankhala could not be made to understand that his approach would have destroyed the whole relationship. The only time Sundari might have attacked would have been from fear; as long as she remained happy and secure, she would remain trustworthy. The leopard was like a wayward, sensitive child who needed direction, but extreme punishments would have only confused her. Solitary confinement for fifteen minutes always brought repentance; she was so socially oriented that to separate her from her family was real punishment. I didn't wish to disregard Mr. Sankhala's expert advice, but I knew his methods were wrong for us. The director, on the other hand, felt that I refused to face reality; he waited with dread for some incident to prove his point.

Searching for some way to lessen the danger, he asked, "If you won't punish her, will you at least restrain her?" I asked him how. "You treat her more like a visiting dignitary than like a member of your family. She has no respect for the needs of others. I'll lend you a harness and chain. You can teach her to walk with you. Take her outside. Let her see and meet people."

Obviously the zoo director had a good point. Sundari was a wild Indian in more ways than one. She wreaked havoc ten times a day in the apartment; perhaps if she was exercised outside, she would be quieter in the house. Yet I hated the idea of displaying her to the general public. Unrestrained curiosity would terrify her. The few times I had taken her in the car we had been nearly mobbed by Indian crowds; no amount of begging could move the aggressively curious throngs away from us. Often at the zoo, Indian visitors had repulsed me with their crude attempts to scare the animals. Uneducated Indians would stop at nothing to make the animals react to their presence. I didn't want to expose Sundari to that kind of behavior.

I agreed to harness her for part of each day, but I refused to name the date when I would first take her outside. I knew Mr. Sankhala was right when he said I was overprotective and indulgent. But I couldn't put her in a situation beyond her capacities.

When I approached her with the harness, she planted her feet wide apart like a bully and dared me to wrap that thing around her. Her attitude was rather like that of a sane person toward a straightjacket: she didn't have to wear it to know she didn't need it. Our ensuing combat made the early bottle brawls look like sparring rounds. This time I wasn't afraid of hurting her—I knew it couldn't be done—but the odds were all in her favor. She weighed in as a twenty-five-pound favorite, nine times her original fly-weight. My own tonnage had remained the same. She had been keeping fit with daily gymnastics while I lolled around laughing at her. She could also leap three times as high as I could and five times as far.

Our battle raged upstairs and down. Murli and Fuzzle took refuge behind kitchen doors; their sympathies lay with Sundari, but the more I panted the more dangerous it was to parade their preferences. Somewhere between the bedrooms and barsati, I realized that I had completely neglected to teach Sundari the first principles of fair play. She not only knocked chairs and tables in my path, but seemed to laugh while I picked myself up. She diverted my attention with broken vases and shattered ash trays. She tangled my legs in the dining room tablecloth. And she knew full well I was scared to chase her along the barsati parapets fifty feet above ground level.

An hour and three bites later, I collapsed on the top step of the barsati to smoke a cigarette and ponder my next move.

Mr. Sankhala was certainly right: Sundari was not afraid of me. But how was I supposed to assert my authority if I couldn't catch her?

With some craftiness of my own, I decided that she fights best who withdraws before her opponent knows she is licked. Then, when the children came home from school, we formed a posse and garnered Sundari in a bathroom. While I held her up by the nape of her neck—and as far away as possible from my person—Kris pinned her forepaws and Rod seized her hind legs. To a chorus of pained yelps and outraged growls, Rob finally strapped the contraption on a very disgruntled Sundari. The deed done, Jan threw open the door. I gave the children time to scatter before I dropped the Cat and ran. Sundari was an agile cub and that afternoon she put on a display of double-jointed calisthenics to rival the act of a circus contortionist. She cut a tornado swath through the apartment, but finally her lower jaw snagged under the neck strap. Before she could injure herself, we had to separate her from the leather. Five of us emerged from the fracas torn and bleeding. Sundari felt too insulted to care about the condition of the rest of us.

The children repaired to a bathroom for first aid, and I went to lie down on my bed for rest and meditation. Her bites were no more ladylike, I figured, than my own swearing, and anyway we had done what we had set out to do: Sundari now knew we could put the harness on her. Authority had been served.

In a few minutes, Sundari slithered out from under the bed and crawled up to massage my neck with her muzzle. She couldn't see the fool harness anywhere so she knew it was safe. Laughing, I put my arms around her. While she washed my face, I thought, "To hell with authority. Who needs it when Sundari loves you?"

In late October, when Sundari was almost five months old, Mr. Sankhala introduced me to the representative of a European zoo—Mr. H., we can call him. "Mrs. Davis has a lovely young female leopard," Mr. Sankhala had told the visitor. When Mr. H. evinced interest in seeing Sundari I asked him to tea. It was always instructive to question people

Rob, Rocky, the Cat at five months, and a harness. Charlotte Bush

who handled large cats, even though I had begun to realize that a house leopard had little in common with those in cages. I especially wanted Mr. H. to see Sundari and give me his opinion on her progress and general appearance.

When he arrived, we sat down to chat while Sundari surveyed him from the bedroom battlements. When she decided the coast was clear, she loped into the living room. She was pretending to be a leopard out for a casual stroll; she stopped in the middle of the room as though surprised to see a stranger. She swished her tail while deciding whether or not she could tease the visitor. Each eyed the other speculatively; then Sundari sensed that this man was not to be trifled with. Quite sedately she took her seat beside me on the couch. Mr. H. had observed her conformation while she looked him over and he commented, "She is beautiful, but you should cut down her food intake." I asked why. "But why do you want her so large? She is too big for her age, and it's not necessary for her to be so well developed," he said.

I still didn't follow his logic. I wouldn't deliberately retard the growth of my children, so why do such a thing to my leopard?

"You misunderstand," said Mr. H. "This is one of the handsomest leopards I have ever seen. Obviously she has good diet and care. But her size—she is as large as a male. The faster she grows, the sooner she becomes dangerous. Why," asked Mr. H., "have you chosen to keep a leopard in your home?"

I tried to explain, but Mr. H. reiterated the opinion of the other authorities: leopards were aggressive, unpredictable, never-to-be-trusted animals—so why have one when a lion or cheetah could be kept with adequate safety? I said quite truthfully that large cats had always fascinated me. I knew that Sundari's advanced development was less due to diet than to the freedom to play and exercise young muscles. I believed that the absence of fear gave her a growth impetus lacking in both wild and zoo animals. And her healthy mental state contributed to her physical condition.

"You may be right," said Mr. H., "but what will you do with her?"

97

I didn't really know, and I didn't want to think about it. "She's still such a baby," I answered, and Sundari put her paw on my leg to assure me it wasn't necessary to worry.

"My zoo would be interested in buying her whenever you are ready to part with her," said Mr. H. "She will be a truly majestic animal when she is grown. An addition to any collection."

"But that would be like selling one of my children," I said.

"Of course," said the visitor, "but the time will come, and soon, when you must face disposing of her. She is already capable of mauling someone severely. It is a matter of days before she will be able to kill."

I was horrified that anyone could consider Sundari capable of killing. She might be physically nearing that stage, but mentally she was not. I assured Mr. H. that she would not harm us, but he insisted, "You don't know leopards. She will turn on you when you least expect it. Mrs. Davis, you have less than one month of safety."

Just then the children came in from school, and Sundari ran to meet them, ready for their usual free-for-all game. She gave them time to drop their books, then leapt onto Rod. In a moment, four young people and one leopard were rolling in a huge tangle, squealing, squirming, arms flying, tail flipping. She took them all on—but she neither bit nor used claws. They were having a wonderful time, as Mr. H. watched in stunned disbelief. "You must stop that sort of play immediately!" he said. "You are teaching her bad habits. She will hurt someone seriously in play!" As he rose to leave, he repeated his offer. "When you wish to make a decision regarding Sundari, contact me through my embassy. I'll be in India another two months."

When he had gone, I sat pondering the distance between our attitudes. My friends accepted my word that Sundari was loving and gentle, but those who regularly handled large cats stridently disagreed. The answer was simple enough. The experts were comparing Sundari with leopards they had seen, but by now Sundari wasn't like any other leopard. While I felt she was exceptional, I knew another leopard would have responded to the same environment in much the same way. Sundari could

98

not have exhibited her high degree of intelligence, adaptability, and charm without the inborn potential. Smart she was, but cunning and crafty she wasn't. Any arguing she had to do she did openly, and she didn't carry grudges. Her rule of thumb about breaking taboos was that you're going to get caught anyway, so why sneak? She was generous with her food, her toys, and her affection. She was never mean and surly, but almost invariably joyful and boisterous. She was not a wild animal or a predator; she didn't need to be. The experts had never observed a leopard's reactions to love and understanding. And yet, it was difficult to remain convinced against all authoritative opinion, and at times I did wonder. Whatever questions I entertained, they didn't stem from distrust of Sundari. They were doubts of my own ability. So I was mindful of the warnings. "We're going to stop the roughest of the wrestling games," I told the youngsters. "And don't let the Cat jump you from ambush."

In unison the children groaned, then openly protested. But I held firm: no ambushing and no rough wrestling. However, those were the only new rules.

"And remember this, all of you," I said. "When Sundari can no longer be trusted, I'll make the decision." It was not a judgment I could share.

During the latter part of November, Bob and I had a chance to take a short holiday in Nepal, our first no-work, no-children vacation in nearly ten years. To us Nepal connoted all the romance of the Orient, and Khatmandu had long been high on our list of places to visit. My Aunt Louise was due for a visit to New Delhi on November 28, so Bob arranged for a driver to pick up the children and take them to Palam Aerodrome to meet their formidable great-aunt. It was no mean feat for a woman in her sixties, who had never before left the continental United States, to travel halfway round the world. Aunt Louise was equal to the mileage, we felt certain, but we were concerned for her comfort.

"Murli, you and Fuzzle must see that our aunt gets a chance to rest the first day," we told the servants. We would return soon, and until then our children could entertain her.

We told ourselves that Auntie would need sleep to recover from jet lag, and that all would be well. As soon as Aunt Louise had invited herself to India, we had written her at length about Sundari. She knew exactly what to expect. "You know I love animals," she had written. Yet I felt uneasy. Aunt Louise, a militant maiden lady, had always been a difficult person.

When we arrived home, my apprehension was confirmed. Sundari had been banished to our bedroom and the children were tense.

"I want nothing to do with that dirty leopard," said Aunt Louise. At the merest mention of the Cat, she left the room like a ship under full sail; Rob then briefed us.

"When we got back home from the airport, we called Sundari to come meet Auntie," said Rob. "They just looked at each other. And then Auntie said, 'Ugh! What do you see in that thing?'

"So,"—Rob was serious, but his eyes had begun to laugh —"Sundari decided to get acquainted by the neck-wash method. She jumped up on the back of the couch, held Auntie down with one paw and started the bath. I never heard anybody yell bloody murder louder, so Rod and I pulled Sundari off. Boy, was Aunt Louise mad. She hollered, 'Lock that thing up!'

"Gosh, Mom, we tried to tell her that Sundari wouldn't hurt her, but she just sulked!"

In spite of Rob's grin, we knew our teen-agers were upset. A hurricane was brewing. The youngsters were torn by conflicting loyalties, and they knew their introduction of Sundari to Aunt Louise had landed their mother squarely in the eye of the storm.

I tried to talk to my aunt, to explain that the Cat behaved that way with everyone who came to see her, to tell her I was sorry she had been frightened. But Aunt Louise wouldn't listen.

"I wasn't frightened—just disgusted. You know I came here just to see the children and to buy some jewels. I did not come to India to be consumed by an ugly monster," she said. "The children are in danger! Really, my dear, it's fortunate I came in time to save them!" Once started, Aunt Louise couldn't stop. "That thing is lethal! It went for my throat immediately!"

I tried to tell her that Sundari only wanted to make friends, that she liked to smell hair.

"It was NOT smelling!" Auntie roared. "Its tongue was on my neck! You don't believe me because you won't listen to anything you don't want to hear, but I'm telling you it tried to KILL me!"

I admitted that Sundari washed necks, too, as her way of getting to know someone. I also explained Sundari's habit of people-pestering. The Cat deliberately annoyed those she could, and when her smart-aleck antics failed, she stopped. But Auntie's aversion was complete. "Here in Delhi Zoo," I told Auntie, "they have a leopard that spent five months with a local family as a cub. It was abused by the children and shut away without human contact. The poor thing is now a complete neurotic. We're not going to do that to Sundari. We simply must not keep her behind locked doors."

"And what about me?" Auntie blurted. "Are you just going to let that thing eat me?"

"No, we'll continue feeding her the usual meals, though maybe we should vary her diet," I answered. Aunt Louise wasn't in the mood for jokes. Neither, however, was I. No one had ever before called Sundari a "thing"—at least not in my presence. I was surprised, too, that Auntie seemed to detest the leopard so violently. Her letters had convinced us that she would enjoy the novelty of living with a leopard. Instead, I now found myself mediating a dispute between an unreasonable old maid and a baby leopard.

Feeling that I must effect some sort of compromise, I kept Sundari in our room part of each day, but not continually. The Cat was confused by a restriction that she considered some kind of punishment. Whenever I entered the room, she gazed at me with hurt, inquiring eyes. Each time I released Sundari, I had to inform Auntie in time for her to barricade herself behind a locked bedroom door. The whole household felt the strain.

Then one evening Bob arrived home from work to find

Sundari still incarcerated. Grandly, he threw open the bedroom door with the flair of a lord chamberlain making way for his queen. To me—not to his aunt-in-law—Bob announced, "The Cat is not to be jailed again! This is Sundari's home," he continued, "and anybody unable to accept that fact can go find other arrangements." In typically masculine fashion, Bob left the explanations to me.

The next few days were a nightmare. Sundari made the most of her freedom while Auntie sulked in seclusion. Sundari had never been locked from any room, and she returned again and again to Auntie's door snuffling at the joints, worrying the handle, trying to understand why the lock would not respond to her jiggling. Such behavior only convinced Aunt Louise that the leopard entertained dastardly intentions upon her person. Finally unable to remain indefinitely in one room, Auntie emerged with the beatified air of saintly martyrdom.

"Just walk in," I urged, "so Sundari won't ambush you." But Auntie wouldn't listen. Worse than that, she persisted in peering from behind partially closed doors. Sundari had played hide-and-seek since infancy so she thought anyone behind a door was there to be pounced upon. The leopard won every game, and sat back on haunches to smile at Auntie's shrill squawks for help—interpreting them as the noise of a poor loser.

Sundari recognized Aunt Louise as an adversary and did her utmost to throw her opponent off balance. In the mornings, when we sat in the sunny breakfast room, Sundari continued to harass Auntie. She would rear on hind legs, rest her forepaws on the table, leer at the unfortunate old lady—simply stare. Other times she sat in front of Auntie, delicately washing her paws; she ogled the maiden lady with hooded eyes. When Auntie began to fidget, Sundari made the "ulping" noises which meant "Look at that!" Aunt Louise stood Sundari's terrorist tactics as long as she could, but after three days she exploded, "When do you intend getting rid of that thing?"

"Certainly not before I have to," I answered. Sundari was sitting on my lap with her nose nestled in my neck.

"It's high time! You should have it put to sleep promptly.

It's going to kill someone. In fact, if you're going to keep that thing, I'll just go home. I refuse to stay in this house with that leopard!"

I was thoroughly exasperated with Sundari for her guerrilla warfare and completely disgusted with my aunt and her infantile ultimatums. For too long I had been the rope in a tug of war between a nit-picking old woman and a gagster young leopard. I jumped up, spilling Sundari from my lap. "You've never given the Cat a chance! You can do what you wish."

And she did. Auntie's proposed two-month visit was cut to two weeks, and when it was over none of us could say we were sorry to see her go. She was the only person who came to our home who failed to fall before Sundari's charm.

But Aunt Louise left behind one interesting legacy. I had asked her to bring along some catnip for the little cats and she had done so. Nuyan and Baby Cat hadn't enjoyed the weed for almost two years, and we wondered how Sundari would react to the plant. When we gave the catnip-stuffed toys to the two sedate Persians, they were transformed into choir boys on a picnic. They groveled on the floor in ecstasy, then turned cartwheels in dazzling displays of acrobatics. They grinned like the proverbial Cheshire cat, and they purred in short-winded chuffs as loud as a locomotive. Their exhilarated intoxication moved them to maudlin fondness for each other and all those around them; their sentimentality even embraced Sundari. But our leopard, unmoved by catnip toys, stared at the performance in awe. Showered with besotted Persian caresses, Sundari was overcome by the magnitude of it all; nevertheless, she greeted their enamored advances with a dignity beyond her months. Politely, she refrained from sneezing as feathery tails fanned her nose. She returned the exotic adoration with moist kisses. At last family regard for her was unanimous. But the hashish of the cat world failed to turn her on—and just as well. There could be few hazards more bizarre than a leopard drunk on catnip.

After Aunt Louise, life quickly returned to normal. We began making plans for a Christmas vacation with a 2,500-mile drive to Goa and back. We intended taking Fuzzle, the cook, and leaving Murli to care for the two little cats. Only one problem beset us: what to do with Sundari. By now we were facing the end of the six-month limitation that the authorities had set for Sundari. She was unaccustomed to cars and couldn't be expected to spend day after day cooped up for so long a ride; we couldn't take her with us. There seemed only three avenues open to us: one, we could send her to the European zoo; two, we could board her at Delhi zoo; or three, we could make provisions for Murli to care for her at home. To dispose of Sundari was unjustified in the light of her affection for us. Like putting a child up for adoption.

The second choice included one attraction. There would be no possibility for Sundari to be harmed. But at the same time, she would be terrified of sights, sounds, and smells unfamiliar to her. She would be fed regularly and well, but no one would play with her, or brush her, or love her. She would not understand what was happening to her or that we were coming back. How could we enjoy the holiday, knowing Sundari was caged and frightened?

After sifting all pros and cons, we decided to keep Sundari at home. We planned elaborate precautions for her safety. Murli handled her well and loved her, as she loved him. We chose the breakfast room as the best place to keep her because it provided the most space with the least furniture for her to destroy. For her sleeping comfort, we purchased a large wicker dog bed and relocated the sandbox from the godown to the breakfast room. The girls padded three new "legs," and we found an old shoe and a worn-out purse to relieve her boredom. Murli was given strict instructions. He was to allow no one access to the house for any reason, and Sundari was not to be allowed to leave the breakfast room. She wouldn't like the confinement, and she would miss the little cats who would have the run of the rest of the house. But she could see them at mealtimes.

With the welfare and comfort of our animals provided for, we loaded baggage onto the car and last-minute instructions onto Murli. Then with light hearts, feeling we were lucky to have so trustworthy a servant, we set off on our trans-India holiday.

7

IT WAS a good Christmas vacation. Bob and I had all four of our children with us—a treat we had not expected to enjoy for a long time. For three weeks we had traveled through central India. We had relaxed on the coast of the Arabian Sea at Goa. We had visited ancient Buddhist temples and rambling Rajput fortresses. Christmas Eve we had spent in a little Maharashtran town where musicians played carols in ragtime and punctuated each stanza with Roman candles. Now, on our way back, we were beginning to long for our own beds and wonder whether our cats missed us.

We were again crossing the Gangetic Plain, and the one-lane road, etched deeply in muddy ruts, stretched flat as far as the eye could see. While I drove, Bob and the children dozed and Fuzzle, still our cook, kept an eye peeled for a banana stand. Half a mile ahead an approaching vehicle flashed its headlights in the Indian signal for right of way, and I looked for a safe place to pull onto the shoulder. Suddenly I realized this was an American government wagoneer signaling me to stop. Pulling over, we recognized the driver and piled out to greet Bhagwan Singh, our friend since the day we arrived in Delhi. "What's the news from Delhi?" Bob asked.

"All is well," said the driver.

"Bhagwan," I asked on sudden impulse, "is Sundari all right?"

"Well," Bhagwan hesitated, "well, memsaahib, she is all right now. I went to the house on Saturday and I could not find Murli but later I saw him, and he told me Sundari had gotten out and he couldn't get her in. But now she is back and you don't have to worry."

I sensed Bhagwan wasn't telling the whole story but I wasn't sure I really wanted to hear it all. We still had five hundred miles to travel and it would take the best part of two days to do it. I just didn't want to know the worst until we could do something about it. We drove on trying not to worry.

The next evening, Delhi lights had been winking in the dark for an hour when we finally pulled up in front of the house. Murli met us at the door. His face was woebegone and frightened, and he was ready to run at the slightest excuse.

"Come upstairs with me, Murli," I said, feeling it best to hear his tale sitting down. And a sad story it was.

On Saturday morning Murli spent extra time cleaning the apartment because he expected us back the next day. He felt sorry for Sundari penned in one room, so he disregarded his instructions to keep her there. She was deliriously happy to be out of confinement. She galloped up and down the steps, turned cartwheels, kissed cats, and searched out Murli himself to rub against his legs in thanks. He allowed her the freedom of the barsati, as usual, but in the alley behind the house two cats started fighting. Sundari went to investigate the struggle, and when Murli called her back into the house she was not to be found on the roof. Later he found her in a tree across the street, but he was unable to entice her down because dogs were circling and barking beneath her and she was too badly frightened. In desperation, Murli went to the zoo

106

with a note I had written Mr. Sankhala for emergency insurance. Zoo people came, knocked her from the tree into a net, and took her away. He pleaded with them, begging on his knees, to leave Sundari with him. They refused. As he finished talking, Murli was crying.

"Murli?" I whispered. "Murli, is she dead?"

"No. She only hurt and she not happy," Murli answered, tears dripping from his mustaches. "Memsaahib, I sorry. I love Sundari; she not bad. She is good leopard. They not understand. They not listen."

"All right, Murli," I sighed. "Make us some coffee and go home. Don't worry any more. If she is alive we'll get her back." I didn't think I could stand any more of the whole story until I talked to Mr. Sankhala.

Nuyan and Baby Cat, delighted to see us, romped around the baggage while I tried to reach the director at his home; but at nine thirty, after repeated attempts, I gave up. In any case, I knew we probably couldn't effect her release before morning. I bathed, sick at heart, knowing that for the first time since she came to live with us Sundari would not be sleeping on our bed beside Bob and me.

In spite of fatigue, I awoke early next morning. I could not call Mr. Sankhala at an inconvenient hour, but I wanted the children to go to school as little upset as possible. Fuzzle appeared to make breakfast, and the two girls from downstairs hurried up to give us the details of Sundari's escapade. They brought us clippings from a Delhi newspaper, complete with a photograph identified as Sundari: eyes smouldering with hate, nostrils flared over drooling fangs, claws extended—the beast was struggling to free itself from half-inch jute mesh. The inaccurate story included such statements as these:

After a dramatic three-hour search in the early hours of Sunday morning, a nine month old pet panther that had been on the prowl since Saturday evening was caught in nets and confined to a cell in Delhi Zoo.

The panther, Sundari, had obviously decided to follow the example of its holidaying master and mistress,

Mr. and Mrs. R. J. Davis of Nizam-ud-Din. But panthers are not allowed to vacation and more so a panther that in the last few months had turned ferocious and unpredictable. From a docile shopping and visiting companion . . . the panther had turned into a snarling angry canine, and therefore, had been confined to the house.

At 6 A.M. on Sunday the zoo squad got out with nets, ropes, sticks and an axe . . . the squad located the panther perched on a thin branch of a neem tree overlooking Nizam-ud Din tomb.

A net was spread on the ground and the branches shaken vigorously. But with the tenacity of a cat the panther clung on. Two keepers gingerly climbed the tree and prodded Sundari with a stick. Scared and nervous, it caught the stick and started climbing towards the keepers. It was only when the branch on which the panther perched was hacked off did Sundari come rolling down. Before the net could be wrapped around it however, it streaked into some bushes nearby. Soon a net was held on one side of the bush and the panther was prodded toward it. The panther tried to rip the net but in the effort found itself emeshed.

Trundled in nets like a new year turkey, Sundari was brought to Delhi Zoo.

Mr. K. S. Sankhala, director of Delhi Zoo, said that if the panther was not restored to its home quickly, it may not be possible to keep it as a pet.

If the animal in the picture was really Sundari, then she did belong to us. I could understand tyros not knowing how to cope with her, but this—this was wanton cruelty practiced by men trained to handle exotic animals. Murli had asked for help, not deliberate destruction; no wonder he had been in tears.

As the children straggled out to meet the school bus, Rod

stopped to kiss me good-bye—an unheard-of procedure. "I'll call you at noon," he said.

When Bob's car arrived to take him to his office, he shook his head. "I think I'll stick around here for a while," he said. He was going to provide reserve support, in case I needed it.

At nine o'clock I called Mr. Sankhala's home and was told he was out of town. Of course, Mr. Sankhala was the only person who could release Sundari, and suddenly I felt strangled by red tape. My friend Charlotte Bush was sure to have heard what happened, so I called to tell her we were home.

"Oh, Rocky, thank goodness you're back," she said. "I went to the zoo, thinking I could comfort Sundari, but she wasn't in the animal hospital. They said they knew nothing about her. What will you do?"

"Well, as a starter I'm going over there," I said. "If she's in the zoo I think I know where. Mr. Sankhala isn't in town but I can't wait for his permission to look for her."

"Do you care if I come along?" Charlotte asked. She didn't want to intrude, but she was ready to lend all support.

"I think two indignant women ought to be more effective than one," I said gratefully.

"Shall I bring along a camera?" she asked. "Or do you think it would upset Sundari?"

"After this, if the Cat is still alive, I don't suppose anything could upset her," I replied.

We rang off, each thinking about the things unsaid. I vowed to bring Sundari home, but quite possibly she could be so deranged by her experience that she would not respond to me. I was filled with apprehension and remorse. When Sundari came home she'd never be left alone again. That much I could swear to.

Rob came down from the barsati bedroom to ask anxiously, "Mom, are you going to get Sundari?" I nodded. "Well, I'd better go with you. You might need me." He meant that he couldn't stand waiting at home wondering what was going on.

I nodded again and told him to be ready in a few minutes. From the picture in the paper we knew that Sundari was in a state of extreme anxiety. Any familiar person and any voice she knew would be a help.

Charlotte arrived, but beyond a few words of greeting, we said nothing on the short ride to the zoo. The gatekeeper didn't want to let us in, but we impatiently waved him aside and drove to a small service lane behind the leopard enclosure. Leaving the car in the middle of the lane, we hopped over a barbed wire fence, crossed a grassy sward, and reached some small cages behind the display pens. How does one distinguish one leopard from fifteen others? It wasn't hard to know mine. Sundari was in the spot I knew she'd be, crouched in a far corner behind a small barricade of straw, shivering and snarling.

"Oh, my God! My God, what have I done to her?" I whispered. Then I called, "Sundari? Oh, Sundari. Pretty? Come, Baby, we're going home."

She rolled her eyes, whites gleaming, unable to focus. Her face was swollen and the silken coat was scabbed with blood. She was thoroughly depressed and had suffered so much she rejected all human overtures. I could hear Rob swearing, not quite under his breath, in a steady stream of language I had never heard him use before. Charlotte stood staring in miserable silence, her eyes filling with tears.

Rob recovered himself first and began crooning to Sundari, the same words over and over, "Sundari? Come on, Baby. It's all right. Sundari?"

Two keepers twittered around us, irritating as gnats, trying to move us away. We brushed them off, making it clear that we would not leave, and continued the singsong stream of encouraging endearments.

Twenty minutes later, Sundari barely moved one ear forward. A familiar sound had penetrated her consciousness. An eternity more, and she cautiously raised herself to a position half-crouch and half-sitting. Her ears were well forward to catch the soft summons of familiar voices. She blinked, then tried to peer at us. She seemed to register an expression of hopeful disbelief. Then she wasn't completely disoriented. She was beginning to respond.

Just then a well-dressed young man rounded the corner. At sight of him Sundari retreated into incoherence. Her defiant snarls reverberated loudly from concrete walls. I had never seen him before, but knew he must occupy some position of authority since the keepers were dancing attendance.

"You will have to unlock this cage and let me in there," I said. I didn't mean to be impolite; I just wanted to get to Sundari before her attention receded again.

"Oh, I can't do that. I haven't the authority," the man replied. "Anyhow, that leopard is dangerous. It has been abandoned."

"Sundari hasn't been abandoned! I'm her mother!" I said. It didn't seem odd to me to claim a leopard as my child. Rob and Charlotte nodded in grim agreement.

"Mrs. Davis? Are you Mrs. Davis?" the young man asked.

"Yes," I said, "and I want Sundari, please."

"I can't let you have her. Mr. Sankhala left strict instructions. Only he can do that. I am Nainand, but I can't help you," he apologized.

"Then let me in that cage. Can't you see she is terrified?" I begged.

"Oh, no! She would kill you instantly! You can't go in there with a wild animal." He was shocked by the very idea. "You don't understand, she isn't tame any longer," he added gently.

"*You* don't understand!" I almost shouted. "I *am* going in there if I have to tear down the walls to do it." I looked around for a crowbar, hammer, maul—anything to begin an assault on the walls. Rob moved in closer, ready to help. Poor Mr. Nainand, trapped by a nearly hysterical woman, flanked by an equally nervous leopard—and still he was sympathetic.

"I'll put it in writing if you wish. I'll absolve the zoo of all responsibility," I shrilled. The sound of our voices had attracted several curious visitors. I was behaving badly, but

I had to make him see what I saw in that cage—a frightened baby animal who needed me. There wasn't time for prolonged explanations.

"All right, Mrs. Davis. I'll let you in." Mr. Nainand knew it would only drag out the scene to argue further, and he asked a keeper to bring the keys.

"Please make those people go away," I said. "I can't do anything while they're gaping at us."

Mr. Nainand considerately complied; he wasn't anxious to treat an audience to the spectacle of a woman being torn to shreds. The door of a nearby cage was unlocked to permit me to crawl through the inner joining doors as the men slid back the panels. The last door finally screeched open, and I spoke softly, "Sundari, here I am. It's all right, Pretty."

But she didn't turn toward me. Instead she eyed the men outside, growling in deep guttural tones. Rob noticed the problem and asked them to move from her line of vision. I eased myself into a sitting position beside the cub, then reached out one hand to fondle her. Startled at my touch, she swung toward me snarling. But in mid-turn the snarl rose to a pitiful scream. She threw herself upon me: thirty pounds of quivering, sobbing leopard landed on my lap. I wrapped my arms about her as tightly as I could to let her know she was safe.

"Sundari? Oh, Sundari, you're all right now. We'll take you home, Pretty," I whispered to her as I held her cheek to mine. "I love you, Pretty. It's okay now." My cheeks were wet with tears as I kissed her broad nose and the downy fur on her muzzle. In my arms she was home already.

She curled into a tight ball on my lap, daintily wrapping her tail around like string on a package. She glared at the cage front defying anyone to come in and separate us. Then turning back to me, she began the ritual of washing my face. I told her what she wanted to hear—that leopard kisses were the very best. And indeed, the best had never been better.

Outside, Mr. Nainand had fully resigned himself to fishing out the pieces. Now his face was an incredulous blank. The keeper's jaw hung slack, the cigarette stuck to his lower lip in eminent danger of scorching him. Neither had ever seen a leopard kissed before. In fact, the sight was so utterly foreign to everything they knew about leopards as to be appalling. Here was a leopard who minutes before had been a screaming scratching banshee; now the men stared in horrified fascination as she licked my face. Rob was clinging to the bars as though he needed their support to hold him upright, and Charlotte, tears streaming, murmured, "Thank God."

"Mom? Can I come in, too?" asked Rob. He didn't remember it wasn't my cage or that he hadn't asked my permission for anything for over a year.

I nodded yes, unable to speak, so my son joined us for paw pats and leopard kisses. Sundari had us all well trained; even in the most trying times none of her family would forget to tell her those kisses were superior. We sat huddled together in the chilly cage, clutching Sundari to us. She could not stop shivering, whether from nervous relief or from chill, I didn't know. But she was safely back from the rim of hell. Rob lit a cigarette which we shared, still crooning nothings to Sundari.

"Well, Mrs. Davis, your leopard is all right now. You can come out." Mr. Nainand seemed convinced he had seen a hallucination and it couldn't last. He wanted us out of there before it collapsed.

"No," I said. "If I leave her now she will think I've deserted her again."

"But you can't stay in that cage," he said. It was really more a question.

"Why not? If it is good enough for Sundari, it will do for me."

"Can't you let Mrs. Davis have Sundari?" asked Charlotte. "Look, you can see she isn't dangerous."

"No, no. There is something about the police. They wanted to shoot her, but Mr. Sankhala wouldn't let them," he answered. "You'd better come out and return when Mr. Sankhala is back from his journey."

"No," I replied firmly. "I will not leave this cage until Sundari does."

113

"But I have some things I must do. I can't stay here with you." Mr. Nainand was upset at the idea of a woman occupying a cell in the zoo, whatever the reason.

"That's all right. We'll just wait for the administration to work things out. You go ahead. We're fine."

"You won't try to take her away?" He had already exceeded his authority by unlocking the cage, and my refusal to leave could earn him severe criticism from his superiors.

"No. I give you my word I will wait," I assured him.

As Mr. Nainand walked away, Rob asked, "So what's to stop us? Mom, you go open the car door and I'll bring her."

"Rob, we can't. I pledged my word. Besides, we wouldn't get as far as the gate before they'd be after us, and we might never get her back. Do you want her kept here?"

"Are you going to just *sit* here?" Rob demanded. At age nineteen, he saw things in sharper perspective than I. To him it was as simple as Sundari belonging to us; no one had the right to detain her against our will. But I knew that the wheels turn slowly in India. To force the issue would only increase resentment and in the long run interfere with our purpose.

"Yes, but you don't have to. You can go home if you want."

"No. If you're staying so am I," he declared. Then he grinned at me, accepting what I said even though he disliked it. Rob had not yet lived in India long enough to know that here patience is not a virtue but a necessity.

The cage was dank and cold. The January sun didn't penetrate thick concrete walls and I shivered beside Sundari. Rob insisted I go out into the sunshine for a few minutes while he held our pet. Charlotte offered me her jacket. While we mapped a strategy of inaction, the leopard rested in Rob's arms, her chin on his shoulder, her eyes closed in weary relief. From time to time, in her fitful sleep, she shuddered convulsively and groaned.

We had only one course of action open to us: to outwait the zoo. If we left the cell, it could take days to arrange

114

her release legally. Sundari was going home—today—but we'd move at India's pace.

As I reentered the cage, Rob came out to stretch cramped muscles, and Charlotte repaired to the office to try to initiate some sort of activity. Several times curious visitors came to stand gawking in at us. Their behavior helped me to understand how miserable a caged animal must feel.

Charlotte returned to say she could still get no information. With only one objective, to get Sundari home where she could be fed and nursed, we felt that we were being deliberately thwarted. We had now spent three hours in a cage.

"The zoo should sell special tickets," Rob said. "To see one leopard and two redheaded Americans all in one cage." It would be a long time before they could present such a novel spectacle for their visitors again.

Time dragged. When Sundari roused, we tried to get her to exercise and prevent stiffness. She drank a little from her bowl of milk. At the time, I saw nothing unusual in that bowl. But in India, where there isn't enough milk for babies, it was a measure of the zoo's concern that milk had been procured for Sundari. At one thirty Mr. Nainand returned to ask me once more to come out, but again I refused. Finally, with real concern, he asked, "Will you bring Sundari to my house where you can wait in dignity? Will you not take her away from the zoo? I can't have you sitting in that cage while I am loose."

He was genuinely shocked at the sight of our sitting in that cell. It deeply hurt his sense of the appropriate. His house was the proper answer; like other zoo executives, he was billeted in an official residence on the zoo grounds. Promising not to abscond, we thankfully accepted his offer. But first Rob would have to go home for the harness, then we would come directly to his house in the car. Mr. Nainand volunteered to tell the keepers where we were going so there would be no misunderstanding.

"My wife will give you some coffee and you will be more comfortable there," he said. "I am going now to have my lunch and will tell her to expect you."

Rob and Charlotte left together. Charlotte had other commitments for the afternoon, and in a dilatory fashion we were progressing in the right direction. At the Nainands' we'd be out of the cage and a half block closer to the gate.

Alone in the cell with Sundari, I reflected on what had happened, but confining walls make for narrow thoughts and squatting in a concrete cave for hours isn't conducive to charitable opinions. She had been abused by men whose very jobs depended upon their ability to handle animals.

Carefully, I examined Sundari's wounds. She had been flayed and stoned unmercifully. Most of the injuries were confined to her face and shoulders, though she was severely bruised in several places on her body. One slash ran from her nose across the left eye and into the ear; while not deep enough to suture, it would leave a scar. At least the eye had been spared. Her lips were swollen, and both upper and lower canine teeth on the right side of her mouth were shattered, as was the lower left. Three upper incisor teeth had been knocked out of her head. Pink serous fluid oozed from her right forepaw, but at first she wouldn't let me inspect it closely. Then I saw that one claw had been completely ripped out of the quick. She was stiff and sore all over. Her injuries were disfiguring, but they appeared superficial. The big question was one of psychology. She was glad to see us and needed us, but could she go home and act as though nothing had happened to her? Obviously, we weren't equipped to handle a leopard that was mentally ill; and Sundari, unlike dogs and house cats domesticated through thousands of generations, possessed no inbred dependence. I wondered whether her veneer of domesticity could endure a thorough beating.

Rob arrived with the harness, and we approached Sundari expecting the usual struggle. But she had now been through too much to protest a minor point. She sensed that we were leaving the cage, and she was no obstructionist. She had only ridden in our car a few times, but it was a familiar landmark. She headed toward it with the fervor of a sinner recognizing salvation, dragging me along behind. Safely inside, she made a tour of the premises, and satisfied herself of its comforts. Then she settled on Rob's knees to look out the windows. For the first time she was alert, interested in her surroundings, and showing no signs of depression. We started down the service road, thankful to put the leopard pens behind us.

Glancing in the rearview mirror, I noticed the zoo jeep jouncing toward us. I hoped this would be the absent Mr. Sankhala, so I stopped. But as the car pulled alongside, one of the assistant directors, Mr. L., jumped out, exclaiming breathlessly, "Mrs. Davis, you really shouldn't do this. It will only make things harder for you." He put his hand on the door but hastily withdrew it when Sundari leaned forward and growled.

"But we're only going to Mr. Nainand's," I explained. "He offered to let us sit at his house and I've given my word to go no farther."

The assistant simply didn't believe me. Apparently guards had been posted to watch us. When we took Sundari out of the cage a report had gone to the main office. Now, this man thought he had caught us with the leopard loot. After nearly six hours in a cage my temper was short. Did he think me so stupid that if I were kidnapping my Cat I would stop to discuss it?

"Whether you believe me or not," I said, "we weren't leaving the zoo, but we are not going back there—none of us will. You'd best report that to your Ministry or whoever is in charge. If we don't soon get permission to leave, we shall all go to your administration offices—or to your homes. We'll wait there. *All* of us."

The message registered.

"Please don't go to the offices. There are some important people there. I'll go for you," said Mr. L., not unkindly.

I shrugged. "We want to go home with Sundari. If we don't see you in half an hour, we'll go there ourselves." We drove on with the jeep following until we turned into the Nainands'.

Though she spoke little English, Mrs. Nainand served us coffee in such a friendly manner that tension began easing away. She was little more than a girl, but she possessed that maternal air which makes Indian women so kind. She clucked softly over Sundari, lying on my feet, and expressed her sympathy by look and gesture. Though I tried to tell her, she will never really know what blessed relief she afforded us that day. Mr. Nainand came in as his wife was pouring second cups of coffee for us.

"The administration has just sent word that you will have to get a court order for Sundari's release because the police were notified." Mr. Nainand looked very apologetic.

Though I wanted to throw something, I set the cup carefully on its saucer. If a court order was necessary at four o'clock in the afternoon, it had also been necessary at ten in the morning. Why couldn't any lackey have told me that?

"How do I go about getting this court order?" I felt suddenly very tired.

"You must go to Nizam-ud-Din police station, and they will tell you how to proceed. I'm sorry, but it shouldn't take more than an hour," he answered. "Your son can stay here with Sundari."

Walking toward the car, Rob assured me that he would do nothing to antagonize anyone in my absence. He'd be polite but firm. He understood that as long as the zoo had legal possession of Sundari, it served no good purpose to let our anger show.

At the police station, I explained my mission to the desk sergeant. The officer found it surprising that anyone should have a leopard and exceedingly odd that once relieved of it they should want it back. But he kindly showed me into the inspector's office. After another explanation, the inspector ordered tea; he then dictated a request for the court order. This document I wrote in longhand and signed. The inspector countersigned it and handed it to a constable with instruction to "make all haste." We settled down to the tea ritual.

"Your leopard caused quite a stir here," the inspector lectured. "You must be very careful it does not happen again." His elbows were on his desk and his chin rested on thumbs while fingers tapped together under his nose.

118

I agreed it must not happen again.

"Why do you keep a leopard?" he asked. "Why not a dog or bird? Aren't you afraid of it?"

"Well, some people charm snakes," I said, "and some enjoy monkeys or dancing bears. I just like leopards." I wondered whether the inspector would ask for a bribe. He did not. As I finished my tea, I remarked that Sundari must be hungry since she hadn't eaten for several days. "I want to get food for her," I said. The inspector was sympathetic.

"I can send the constable to the zoo when he returns with the court order," he volunteered.

I stopped at home for Sundari's cooked meat, then hurried back to the zoo. The trip had taken less than an hour, but Rob was waiting anxiously at the road edge. Sundari was sitting quietly beside him.

"I've had an awful time," he said. Sundari had jerked at the lead, jumped on furniture, growled at Mrs. Nainand, and in general displayed all the unwholesome symptoms of a tired spoiled child. She had misbehaved from the moment my car had disappeared until she heard the engine returning. She had been so wild Rob had removed her to the garden. There she had crushed chrysanthemums, chased chipmunks, and charged passing pedestrians. Rob concluded his account with the opinion that he'd better run the errands and leave the leopard to me. Despite his chagrin I couldn't help snickering at the picture of innocence she was presenting, happily licking my legs.

Mr. Nainand invited us into the house again, and I sat on the floor feeding Sundari from my hand as we chatted. He marveled at the miracle he had witnessed during the morning. He had helped capture her, had never seen a cat fight so furiously, and wondered why we tolerated so wild an animal in our home. Her behavior in the zoo had done nothing to make Mr. Nainand revise his opinion. She had rejected all overtures, refused to eat, scared the keepers—a true demon among leopards. He had handled many animals and thought he knew something about them; he had believed her a total loss.

"Why," I asked, "if you really thought she would kill me, why did you unlock the cage?"

"Sundari had no other chance for survival," he said. "And you were so determined, Mrs. Davis." So a demon had turned into a kitten before his eyes.

By seven thirty in the evening the constable had not appeared, and Rob, worried that something had gone wrong, decided to go to the police station to look for him. An hour later he returned with the constable in tow and the court order ready for delivery to the acting chief of the zoo. Mr. Nainand walked to the office, but, like the director, the acting chief himself was away on an errand.

We sat back to twiddle our thumbs. It was late and we were weary but, with food, Sundari had regained some of her impish impulses. Mrs. Nainand brought more coffee, and when several relatives wandered in, Sundari sat jiggling on my lap making the "ulping" sound she used to show me something. She looked at me to ask whether she should give them the benefit of some charm, leopard style. I applied a little pressure on her shoulders, persuading her to lie down rather than misbehave. Meantime, Mr. Nainand and the constable spoke in Hindi, a conversation I followed with difficulty. We had occupied the Nainands' living room for five hours, and I felt it was an imposition, though they both protested it was not. The constable very uneasily eyed Sundari while she watched him closely. From the security of my lap she was debating the advisability of scaring him properly; finally she decided in favor of discretion. Under normal circumstances she enjoyed her practical jokes, and now that she was fast recovering her poise, I fervently hoped we could get her out of the house before she pulled off a practical catastrophe. However, she contented herself with needling the constable, making a soft hissing sound with the tip of her tongue between her teeth. Her nose was ever so slightly wrinkled showing only a hint of gleaming fangs. It was the closest she could come to thumbing her nose and that was just what she meant by the gesture. Her head was tilted to one side so that she looked at him directly but from the corners of her eyes and

120

with each sound of *theess, theess,* she bobbed her head up and down.

The constable suddenly cleared his throat: "You can take the panther home now. I have the necessary papers in my briefcase. The signature is only a formality."

I was hard put to keep a straight face. He obviously entertained serious reservations about sitting so close to a leopard who made faces. Mr. Nainand paled at the idea. I, however, declined to act. We would wait for official sanction to go; I wouldn't take a chance on something going afoul now.

A knock at the door brought word at last that the acting director had returned to the zoo grounds. Rob went with Mr. Nainand and the constable for the required signature while I gathered up Sundari's things and once more tried to thank Mrs. Nainand for her kindness. When they returned, Rob's expression was so grim I thought it must be bad news, but he slid behind the wheel and said simply, "Get in! Let's go home."

"It's done," said Mr. Nainand. He was smiling. "You can go, Mrs. Davis. I'm sorry you had so much trouble."

Sundari hopped into the back seat, and I climbed in beside her.

"We can't thank you enough," I told Mr. Nainand. "I hope your hospitality didn't get you into too much trouble with your administration."

Mr. Nainand smiled ruefully. "Well, there has been a bit of difficulty, but it was worth it. I've seen a miracle."

We shook hands warmly, and Rob drove off, down the dark lane with its cages of sleeping animals, then through the gates into the city streets. We drew a deep breath of free air. We were out at last.

Without looking at me, Rob burst out bitterly, "Do you know who had to sign that court order? The same man who led that bunch of thugs—the men who clubbed Sundari. He admitted it! He sneered at me, and said, 'I guess you think I mistreated your pet. Well, we didn't kill her!' Mom, I wanted to belt him in the teeth!"

"And what *did* you do?"

"You said to keep my mouth to myself, so I just said, 'No,

sir, we don't think anything. My mother is tired and I want to take them home.' Then he signed the receipt."

I tried not to let him see my smile. For the first time in his life, Rob had curbed a powerful impulse in order to gain his ends. Throughout our long day he had fumed, but he had learned a lesson in self-restraint he would not soon forget. Then, without even realizing it, he had quietly taken command of the situation. Thanks to a six-month-old leopard, Rob had that day become an adult.

8

IT WAS 10:45 P.M., January 5: a New Delhi night cold enough to require a blanket. Brittle-bright stars, somehow closer in dry season, glittered prismatically in the night sky when Sundari came home from the zoo for the second time. Inside the door, she took the steps six at a time, groaning her excitement. Her tail banged the walls as it swept wide arcs in the air. If we had entertained any doubts about where she belonged, Sundari herself had none at all. Before Rob and I made the first landing, she was in the living room greeted by wild shouts of welcome. Family and servants alike milled around her to get close, to touch her so that they knew she was really there.

"Sundari! You're home!"

"Memsaahib, she here—*voo yāahāa hai!*"

"Mom! She's hurt."

"What took you so long? We've been waiting."

"*Sundari, aap achii cheetah-billi hai*—Sundari, you're a good leopard."

"She's shivering, she's cold."

"No, she's hungry!"

For once the servants joined us with no self-conscious thought of position. Murli and Fuzzle touched Sundari before retreating to the doorway, smiles splitting their seamy faces in half. Our beloved Cat was home. Bob, never demonstrative, sat on the couch with a grin smeared from ear to ear. The children crowded around her noisily. Nuyan circumspectly withdrew, but Baby Cat surveyed the show through slitted eyes from the stereo cabinet.

Fuzzle ran to get me hot coffee as I dropped into a chair. I still had one more official stop, but I needed to relax for a minute first. Rob could fill in the details of our day while I went on to the police station to sign the charge sheet. I called Charlotte to let her know we were home. Meantime, Sundari lay in the middle of the floor lavishing kisses and patting everyone she could reach. Those missed with paws got caught by her sweeping tail.

With my coffee Fuzzle brought a dish of ground buffalo for Sundari. Between huge gulps of meat she ran from person to person, reassuring herself that she was safely back where everyone adored her. In the middle of her meal, she remembered the cats. She ferreted Nuyan from his lair with one paw and dealt him the most meaningful scrub of his lifetime. Nuyan, freshly laundered, beat a hasty retreat while Sundari looked for Baby Cat. Spying him on the stereo, she swatted him off and held him securely to the floor to wash him. He protested vociferously, but soon sparkled moistly clean. Despite their annoyance, Sundari didn't hurt either cat and when it was over, she shared her dinner with them.

Though she was not as wildly boisterous as she had been, her every movement expressed relief and happiness. To see her reenter family life so whole-heartedly helped to lessen our fears. But to Rob and me, Sundari's about-face from the morning seemed almost psychopathic. Would she harbor resentments that might one day erupt unexpectedly? And if such a thing happened, could we act in time to avert disaster? I preferred to put my faith in the animal rather than speculate about the future. Hadn't our Cat always been different?

At the police station, I signed a document I could not read because it was written in Persian script. Saying good night, I started for the door too tired for hurry. I was halfway down the steps when a voice stopped me: our friend the constable called, "Mrs. Davis, don't you want to see the inspector before you go?"

I didn't really. What purpose was there in seeing the inspector unless to haggle over bakshish? But in the interest of neighborhood peace, I retraced my steps, and the constable pleasantly ushered me into the tiny office cubicle. The inspector, tousle-haired and wearing pajamas under his overcoat, was seated at his desk, but the rumpled blankets on his charpoy showed he had risen in haste.

"Will you take tea?" the inspector asked kindly.

"No, thanks," I said. "I just stopped to thank you."

"Please sit down. Is Sundari all right?"

The inspector had learned the leopard's name—and he wasn't after a gratuity at all. Ours was such an unusual case that he wanted to learn its conclusion. He could tell his grandchildren about it, how he had taken part in the glorious capture of this animal, and then of its return. Several men in uniform drifted in to listen to our conversation, to see me and to decide what sort of woman would live with a leopard. "What will you do with her now?" my host continued.

"For the moment we will love her and hope for the best," I said. "She's like a child. She has suffered a terrible experience."

"Are you not afraid? What of your children?" he asked.

Again that question of fear. Almost everyone asked that question, and I couldn't understand the reason. What sort of people would keep an animal they feared? Suddenly I realized we were freaks. Fair-skinned, red-haired, a family from a foreign country with a completely different background. Perhaps in America people did keep pets they feared.

"No," I answered wearily, "we aren't afraid of her. She

would never hurt the other children. We are her family and she has been raised as though she were our child, too."

The concept was new and the night stretched long before the inspector. He wanted to pursue it, chew it over, discuss it from every angle before the sun rose. He understood children, but how could a wild animal be considered in the same light? He shook his head to clear it of sleep and prepared for a long session. Had the hour been eleven in the morning I might have chatted, but I was too exhausted. I thanked him again and asked him to call on us someday. Then I fled through the door.

In bed with Sundari's bulk pinning the covers between Bob and me, the whole day seemed less than real. That she could have survived such an ordeal and retained her confidence in us wasn't likely. After all, she was a *wild animal*. Everybody said so. That newspaper picture in the *Times of India* showed a typically feral cat. But here she was snuggling close to me, taking her half of the bed from the middle. It just couldn't be, but I went to sleep with my arms around a leopard and Sundari's nose nuzzling my cheek.

Usually when Sundari hit the sack she was good for eight hours, but that night she roused us time and again, sandpapering our faces and arms and necks with her tongue. Whether she was reassuring herself or us I don't know, but in the morning Bob and I agreed that her strenuous attentions left us little time for sound sleep. We also found that a lot of food doesn't go very far in a healthy young leopard. Sundari's three-kilo intake of the previous night had not dented her morning appetite. She ate a one-and-a-half kilo breakfast and returned to her pad to sleep it off. While she slept I did some thinking.

The blame for Sundari's escapade was rightly mine. I should have known better than to leave her. Had I really considered her needs above my pleasures, she would never have gotten herself into the predicament. Perhaps I should have explained to Murli my reason for not wanting her on the barsati: I knew she could jump off it if she wanted. But it wouldn't have mattered. An illiterate simple man deals in realities, not possibilities. Murli would have seen only what he did see: a lonely and bored pet. He wasn't able to foresee the consequence of disobeying explicit orders. He was there and we were not, so Sundari could have a romp, with no one the wiser. He had never had difficulty handling her before. His judgment carried him no farther. He had been wrong to ignore instructions, but in one respect he had been entirely correct: the zoo didn't understand.

Sober reflection brought home the fact that zoo keepers were no more equipped to handle Sundari than police. Men trained to handle exotic animals in cages are not necessarily able to handle them in another situation. To zoo personnel a leopard—any leopard—is a potential threat to life. If loose, it must be captured and subdued. They didn't know how to entice Sundari home, but that wasn't their fault.

"If Murli had just propped open the door downstairs," Bob opined, "if he'd stayed upstairs, Sundari would have come in right away." Bob was right. She was not an escapee in the usual sense; she only wanted to get home. Badly frightened to begin with, she faced the hullabaloo created by police, zoo men, dogs, and thrill-seekers. Her terror increased. Too late she learned her lesson: other pastures may not be green at all.

But there was another matter. Sundari had been raised as a human child, petted, pampered, adored, rarely scolded. The household was organized around her needs and capabilities. We knew she was an intelligent, sensitive animal and we acted accordingly. Young animals, like human children, learn their lessons in social behavior by the example of their elders. Animals are not born with full knowledge about the mores of their society. They are taught, their instincts are developed by maternal zeal. Sundari, a leopard by spots and a human by inclination, had been taught love. That was all she had ever known until she found herself up a tree, surrounded by a bloodthirsty howling horde. Nothing in her background had prepared her for such a circumstance, and in her terror she reacted in the only way she could, with claws and fangs bared. Most humans, facing the same odds, would not react so bravely, nor would they be fortified with the courage to forgive as she was. On one point I felt quite certain: rather than consign Sundari to the life of a zoo animal, I would have her destroyed.

But reflecting further, I realized there was still unfinished business to attend. First, I wrote Mr. Sankhala a long letter so that when he returned he would know I in no way blamed him for our misadventure. I particularly wanted to tell him how kind the Nainands had been to us.

To the *Times of India* I wrote: "Your reporter stated, '. . . in the past few months has turned into a ferocious and unpredictable. . . .' I would be deeply grateful to know just who presented that lie. . . ." I quoted again, " '. . . had turned into an angry snarling *canine* . . .' For your reporter's edification, a canine is a dog or a tooth. Sundari is not now, never has been, and will not be a canine. She is a feline. . . ." And so on. If I spread little enlightenment, the letter made me feel much better.

Three days of fasting had done Sundari no permanent damage, and her wounds were not deep, but she was exhausted mentally and physically. After her ordeal, she spent the first three days resting on our bed and left it only for food and the sandbox. She displayed deep affection for us, but showed no interest in her favorite pastimes of bird-watching and people-teasing. She was not the blithe creature we had known— though she was easier to live with. We found no broken flower vases, chewed pillows, or smashed water bottles. Her zest for life seemed spent, we feared permanently. After eating to immobility, she slept off the surfeit like a person after Thanksgiving dinner.

By the fourth day, though, her rest cure began to work. She perked up and commenced looking for messes to make. On the fifth day she found them. She rollicked back into her old habits. The day she sent me sprawling with a fast paw between the legs I was overjoyed. Within a week she had recaptured her vivacity. "We didn't know when we were well off," Jan complained. The only scars remaining were psychological— and they were ours. Sundari had more heart than we; and her confidence in us was so great that she had recovered completely.

128

One evening after the boys had expelled her from their room complaining, "She can't play Monopoly," Sundari clomped down the steps and threw herself into her basket-bed. The bedding heaved. A squeal of resentment exploded beneath her, and Nuyan clawed his way out from under. But with a smile to prove that she really hadn't meant to disturb him, Sundari scooped up the Persian with one paw and cuddled him to her chest until his anger subsided. Poor Nuyan, whose coat was so thick and heavy that he always preferred to sleep alone, had to wait till Sundari's regular breathing signaled it was safe to leave.

Sundari put that basket to other uses, too. Flipped on its side, she could roll it like a hoop. One good swat sent it spinning into the backsides of passersby. Confronted with the evidence, the culprit daintily washed her paws. Her innocent, sloe-eyed glance asked how we could possibly think her guilty when all the time she had been busy with her toilet. Besides, what sort of leopard went around throwing her bed at people?

From one of his trips to Iran, Bob had brought me a string of camel bells. These the boys had confiscated and rigged up for their room with an arrangement of pullies and sash cord. The bells could be rung from anywhere in the stairwell as a step-saving summons. Sundari discovered she could keep all of us scurrying like so many mice with one good yank after another. She wisely tried her trick from different levels so that it was several days before we caught her. By that time the boys had been warned against summoning Murli when they didn't want him; their friends had been told that excessive noise was not welcome in our house. Fuzzle was informed that the bells were for our exclusive use. In fact, Murli and Sundari were the only ones not suspect. Murli would never have run himself ragged up and down the stairs. Sundari finally blundered. She snagged a claw in the cord and was still trying to free it as I came up the steps. But she wasn't repentant. She smirked, waggled her whiskers, and swished her tail in a self-satisfied manner. She knew that we'd forget and the trick would work again.

One afternoon, our friend the neighborhood constable

came to call on Sundari. He brought along a friend, another constable. Both visitors seemed to have deep, wracking coughs that only a straight shot of Scotch could relieve. It was pleasant to find the police so concerned for the leopard's welfare, for they had seen her in her one worst moment. Even though we knew they had come out of curiosity to see how we lived, we were honestly delighted at the visit. Neither man became entirely at ease in Sundari's presence; each sat on the edge of his chair, his cap in hand, ready to leap away at the least provocation. We kept our eyes peeled for signs of mischief on the Cat's part. It might be helpful to have sympathetic police nearby. Perhaps Sundari sensed our mood; she seemed to know that these were moments for discretion.

About a week later, I received a call from a gentleman identifying himself as Mr. R., a writer from the *Junior Statesman*. Could he call on Sundari and interview me? Still smarting from our last public exposure, I rather abruptly said no, thanks.

"But you misunderstand!" protested Mr. R. He explained that he had heard of Sundari from a friend of Bob's. He had heard nothing about our press problems. His magazine, a weekly for young people, simply wanted a feature story about us. "If you let us do it, an article could allay any anxiety in your neighborhood." He had a point. I agreed to let Mr. R. and a photographer come along.

The journalists arrived in good order and after they were seated in the living room, I called Sundari. She had been keeping a silent surveillance from behind the bedroom ramparts. She minced into the room in a clumsy kitten imitation of a ballerina; she wore the smug smirk of coming deviltry. Her whiskers sagged languidly, and her lids drooped over coppery irises. But in spite of her indifferent air, anyone who knew her could recognize signs of impending disaster.

Uneasily, I fed her cheese tidbits, followed by a lagniappe of Junior Ham, and put her through company capers for the camera. To keep her mind from plotting against our visitors, I tried to keep her attention on food. When the routine exhibition was over, we turned to improvisation. Sundari was nothing if not inventive.

Smiling charm radiated from her whole swaying body as she sidled up to Mr. R. By now, after a half hour with Sundari, he was relaxed and as self-confident as an Asian Frank Buck. Not so his sidekick. The photographer's spine was glued to the back of our green chair; his feet were ready for flight. As Mr. R. leaned forward to return Sundari's grin, he reached out a tentative hand to stroke her forehead. Sundari then brought her press conference to a close.

She grasped Mr. R.'s knee between her canines and slid them down his calf all the way to the ankle. She exerted just the right amount of pressure to avoid tearing his trousers. The result was spectacular. As she released his ankle, the poor man catapulted from his seat and made a dive for the stairs. After the door slammed, he called back that he'd be in touch. The photographer had preceded the writer all the way.

"Sundari! You really shouldn't!" I told her. "Your judgment is awful."

But I couldn't keep a straight face. She rested her chin on my lap, gazing up at me with a smile that said, "I'll do it again, and you'll be rolling in the aisles when I do."

9

TWO WEEKS after Sundari's debacle with the zoo, her shattered tooth grew infected. She willingly let me inspect it, the right lower canine, as soon as she felt secure again. I had assumed that while she would have some discomfort masticating, the broken teeth were only cosmetically disfiguring. Her food was already ground so she did not need the canine for ripping and tearing meat as she would have under normal circumstances; the jagged edges would soon wear smooth.

But then we noticed a painful swelling in the jaw just below the tooth. I could have started antibiotics immediately, but I hesitated since I didn't know the correct dosage. Besides, I wanted to delay treatment a day or so to see what developed. The Cat had never been ill and otherwise was in good condition; her system might well throw off the infection without aid. In retrospect, it seems ridiculous that I did not give her medical attention straightaway. The little cats never had to wait, but Sundari seemed so different. In any event, I could not decide what needed doing until the swelling and tenderness subsided.

The next two weeks justified all the faith we had in Sundari. I still marvel at her fortitude. Miserably uncomfortable, she would come to lay her aching jaw on my thigh or cupped hand; body warmth apparently eased the pain. She seemed to know that my probing fingers were meant to help; she only winced when I touched the painful spot. She was eager for comfort, and huddled close whenever I sat down. She discontinued her daily galloping games because bouncing aggravated the pain, but she remained gentle and congenial with the family and the cats.

For three days the swelling ballooned until she looked like a defeated boxer. Then I decided that a five-day course of penicillin could no longer be postponed. Pure guesswork determined that the dosage should be the same as for a six-year-old child. Sundari weighed thirty-two pounds, far less than a child of six, but a little too much penicillin was better than too little. By the evening of the second day of treatment, the massive swelling began to abate; by the following morning progress was obvious.

As the swelling receded, a gum boil developed in the mucous fold between her jaw and the inner lip. If the infection had localized, I reasoned, the penicillin would effectively take care of it. However I had read that leopards retained their milk teeth for two years; inevitably we would have many recurrences unless the offending tooth was removed. The closer Sundari's jaw approached normal, the nearer I came to a difficult job: I would have to pull her tooth. My only consolation was that if I survived the operation, I would enjoy the distinction of being the world's only living leopard dental surgeon.

Armless, perhaps.

In times of stress, human minds often focus on trivialities rather than realities. Certainly that was true in my case. Instead of trying to acquire some dental forceps, or learning what to do if the tooth broke, I just assumed that all would go well. I knew not to risk an anesthetic because felines require such large quantities to knock them out—there is a fine feline line between stupor and infinity. It was a measure of my quackery that the use of tranquilizers didn't occur to me. It should have. Nuyan and Baby Cat had been tranquilized for their journey to India, and they had arrived relatively calm.

The gum boil gave far less discomfort than the swelling that had preceded it, and as Sundari became more active I felt less eager to extract her broken tooth.

Seven days after the swelling had first appeared, an angry gray-green knob capped the boil. Lancing it would be the proper preliminary to extraction. The sheer lunacy of my plan still hadn't dawned on me. But as I sterilized a sewing-machine needle, I recalled a fragment of that line from Tennyson: "Into the jaws of hell. . . ."

I arranged my instruments: the sterile needle, Q-Tips dipped in vodka, cotton—and with more nerve than sense, I approached Sundari. She was lying on our bed. Easing down beside her, I lifted her head between my hands and kissed the muzzle softer than eiderdown. Was this to be the last time she would grunt contentedly at the touch of my hand? After seven months of rapport, was I about to destroy her trust? "Oh, Sundari, I'm so proud of you," I said. "Don't let me down now. I'm doing the best I can."

For answer, she rolled on her back, her emerald-copper eyes smiling as they always did when she awakened. Taking her head in my lap, I swabbed at the jaw with a Q-Tip. With a lucky deftness born of panic, my needle jabbed into the eye of the boil. Opalescent green pus roiled out in thick snaking coils, spilling over my hand and the spread. After an involuntary jerk, Sundari's head relaxed on my lap. The crater oozed putrid opaque fluid, but Sundari did no more than flick her tail. I cradled her head in my arms while tears of relief streamed down my face. In that moment she was more precious to me than she had ever been. We were a month past the "safe" period that the authorities had set; yet, after all the turmoil she had experienced, this seven-month-old leopard had allowed me to lance a boil with more cooperation than a child would have given. Once again she had proved herself the one best expert on leopard behavior.

Well into the second month of "it can happen anytime," an American zoologist visited Delhi. He was curator of one of the most progressive zoos in the United States, and I welcomed the chance to get his opinion. He listened to my account of Sundari and then advised, "Get rid of her as soon as possible. No western zoo will want a damaged leopard. They're too easy to come by. If you can palm her off in India, you'll be well rid of her." Then he added, "Leopards adjust easily because they haven't any depth. Lots of people have raised them to three or four months and when they part with the animals, the cats don't even miss the owners."

He had failed to note that I wasn't looking for a way to place her. He had not considered Sundari's feelings because he didn't know she had any. I had intended asking him to see her, but his words convinced me it would do no good. This was the last time I asked for expert guidance. Too many of the authorities were simply professionals who happened to deal in animals; their wares might as well have been light bulbs. They believed in handling beasts with the care that any investment deserved, but it was a shock to learn that they hadn't any *love* for the animals. None of the three authorities had raised a great cat in their homes.

It was time and past to quit asking for advice based on faulty experience. None of the authorities I consulted had realized that my fears were never *of* Sundari, but always *for* her. Today I wonder why, for so long a time, I was so sure of my Cat and so unsure of myself. Once I threw off the shackles of uninformed advice, we settled into a deeper and more secure relationship. Had I not come to grips with myself, I doubt that Sundari would have been able to stay with us.

The jaw healed well, but I postponed the extraction because of my ignorance of dentistry. I vividly remembered my own pain at age five when a dentist parted me from a baby tooth without benefit of anesthetic. While I was dithering over procedure, I noticed a tiny wen on the gum immediately behind the bad tooth. Another had appeared in a similar position on the left side. Was it possible these were secondary teeth about to erupt?

All the information I possessed indicated a totally different age and pattern of eruption. The same oracle who averred that leopards couldn't be raised on buffalo meat had also written that "adult teeth erupt into the hollow baby teeth at age two years. As the second teeth grow, the milk teeth begin to dissolve and eventually slough off. In this manner the leopard is never without fangs for catching, ripping, and tearing the flesh of its prey." It all sounded so convincing and logical. Had Sundari been within six months of the magic age of two, I might have thought her simply precocious once more. But a sixteen-month discrepancy was too great for individual differences in the same species. At least, I could postpone surgery until we could determine whether or not my suspicions were correct.

Common sense might have dictated that Sundari would make no effort to leave the house again, but we took no chances. I would not allow her on the barsati. Terrified she would get away and be killed, I kept the door to the barsati shut and locked at all times. Yet I knew we could not provide the necessary play room inside the house. Therefore, like it or not, Sundari would have to go outside. The prerequisite for any outdoor excursion was a suitable harness. With measuring tape and drafting paper, I worked out my own engineering design. At a local leather shop I asked the craftsmen to make two—the second harness for emergency use. Once we put the harness on her, Sundari was going to wear it all the time. As a permanent uniform, it must be both comfortable and foolproof. It consisted of adjustable neck and body straps connected by a wide band running between her shoulders, so that she could pull backward or forward but be unable to slip out of the contraption.

While we waited for the harness maker to complete his work, Sundari was forced to use the sandbox once again. She accepted the demotion with the same grace she did all my whimsies, but she did have difficulty covering her feces. She couldn't keep all four feet in the box and cover at the same time. She always got at least one paw dirty. One afternoon Rob and I watched as she stepped out of the box and prepared to cover her movement. Murli happened along and stopped to pat her head. The Cat looked up at him with such wide-eyed,

136

imploring dependence that he couldn't resist. Bending over he scooped sand over the mess with one hand; with the other he fondled her head murmuring, *"Bus, bus, Sundari. Thiik hooga."* She sniffed at the heaped sand with a grimace and lifted her paw to finish the work. But Murli responded, patting a trifle more sand on the mound to suit the queen. She then kissed his free hand and swayed off regally. Murli folded his arms and grinned after her, proud to have been of service.

"Mom! You wouldn't have believed that if I'd told you!" Rob gasped. But I would have. Our untouchable Murli, the unclean, the illiterate man whose very shadow would defile one tenth of the Indian population, understood our Cat.

Each day I inspected Sundari's gums. Finally, my finger tips confirmed our suspicions: in spite of leopardologist assertion, the small lumps had erupted into nascent white teeth— sixteen months early. No extraction was necessary.

With this good news came more. Mr. Sankhala had returned; he had read my letter and wanted to confer with me. Could I join him for coffee in his office next morning?

Mr. Sankhala, genial as ever, welcomed me in his old friendly manner. We talked of his cats and mine, of what had happened and why. "It was terrible," said Mr. Sankhala. "One of my best men told me, 'I've never been so afraid of any animal before.' But then, I've always told you that she is not afraid of people."

"What else could be expected?" I asked. "She'd never had a cross word spoken to her. She's a baby, and all her normal props were gone."

"She must not have acted like a baby," said the zoo director. "She isn't domesticated, and she is no longer an infant. I beg of you, watch her every minute!"

"I will," I said, though my answer was noncommittal. We had been all over this ground before. But Mr. Sankhala couldn't let the subject drop. "Are you still sleeping with her?" he asked.

"Yes," I said, "she's afraid of the dark by herself."

"You make fun now, but how can I convince you that you are not safe with this leopard?" he demanded. I told my friend

137

it wasn't possible. "Will you promise not to turn your back on her?"

"No," I said. "I'll turn my back, I'll sleep beside her, I'll put my face next to hers. I'll let my children and my cats play with her and I'll feed her from my hand until the day we have to part. No one on the face of this earth will ever make me afraid of her."

I had raised my voice, and now Mr. Sankhala thundered, "Mrs. Davis, you will die by that animal!"

His concern was as deep as his feeling of outrage. After I left him that day, I tried to reason out the nature of our quarrel. More than once Mr. Sankhala had called me his protégé. What happened to turn the master against his apprentice? Was it simply two cultures in a head-on clash? My background emphasized equality among men and variety in self-expression; we accept animals easily and with few barriers, as individuals. But India's traditions and religion create insurmountable barriers. The Hindu philosophy of caste sets one man above and apart from another, and all men above other creatures—except for the sacred cow.

The new harness finally arrived. With the usual struggle, Rob and I strapped it onto the protesting Sundari. Before we added the lead, however, we let her wear the harness and get used to it. Too many innovations at once would only confuse her. Until she was nine months old, Sundari had worn her ill-fitting first harness perhaps a dozen times. This time, surprisingly, she accepted the new rig with far less agitation than we expected. She whined and butted, did some fancy somersaults, and tried to pull off the belly strap with her teeth. But these tricks seemed more like devices to get attention than a serious effort to get loose. In one day, she had forgotten the harness entirely and wore it without concern.

The next Sunday, while Bob puttered in the walled garden, I took up the chain and asked, "Want to go out?"

Indeed she did! No part of the feline anatomy is more expressive than the backside; Sundari's swayed up the stairs like a small boat anchored against a strong tide. At the door I clipped the chain to the harness and we lurched past the

138

screen. Bob looked up from his vulnerable flower beds with horror. Obviously, he regarded us as on a par with an invasion of grasshoppers or a plague of plant virus. Raising his eyes to the firmament, he muttered something that sounded like "My God! The botanical Carrie Nations!"

Sundari and I were making highly uncoordinated progress. We couldn't seem to get aimed in the same direction at once. After five minutes of dragging my hundred pounds behind her, Sundari was so disgusted that she slammed her rump on the floor and flatly refused to budge. For which Bob offered thanks.

In the next four days we successfully devastated two months' worth of Bob's gardening work. Most of our difficulty came when Sundari and I tried to get around the flower pots; we were rarely on the same side of one at the same time. She would spend long minutes lunging against restraint; then she would balk and in plain snarls tell me what she thought of the whole affair.

I tried to get her interested in something to take her mind off the chain so that she would stop struggling. Rob hauled the stepladder to the middle of the floor where it wouldn't hit pots if it tipped over and where I could circle it as she played on the rungs. As soon as she saw her toy fish and a Clorox jug on the top she raced to get them—ignoring the lead.

Using toys and the ladder as our props, we were able to handle her for longer and longer periods and give her the exercise she needed so badly. We were still a long way from providing adequate exercise for a healthy young leopard, but we had come a long way.

Mr. R. called me one evening in late February to say that the *Junior Statesman* with the feature about Sundari would be on the stands the next morning. His story was warmly sympathetic. And he had graciously refrained from mentioning his own hasty exit from the house. For the first time Sundari was presented to readers as we wished—as part of the family.

Sunday was the servants' day off. On Saturday the cook usually prepared a roast of meat which we consumed next day between slabs of homemade bread. One Sunday afternoon, Jan

put the roast and bread on the counter before she went to get her father to carve. Before they got to the kitchen a terrible uproar began. Sundari had stumbled across a free meal. She was there alone growling like thunder. Next, she whisked it to the top of the cabinets, and from her perch the guttural growls made it clear she had no intention of parting with her prize.

"Okay, Sundari," I said, "it's all yours." I closed the door and left her to the stolen fruits. It would have been foolhardy to attempt to take it away with her in that frame of mind, and rather than risk a confrontation that she might well win, I let her have it. A Sunday on tunafish sandwiches wouldn't hurt us, but did Sundari's manner indicate the beginning of the end?

She hadn't made a move toward me; she had only warned me off. I knew that all cats, hungry or not, will sometimes steal meat. I couldn't think of any cat who wouldn't put up a fight to keep his ill-gotten gains. So I regarded my action not so much as retreat but as a way to avoid backing down. Jan had lived with cats long enough to know better than to leave meat out, and we would have to see that no similar opportunity occurred again. The next time, the consequence could be disastrous.

In India, March is the month when the walls seem to sprout baby lizards. It is also the month when our cats concentrate a whole year's activity into thirty days of lizard-chasing. Our geckos were not things of beauty—stubby, pinkish-beige, and warty. But at the sight of these reptiles, the cats leapt to life. Even idle thoughts of lizards excited them; we could point to a bare spot on the walls and whisper, "Look, Nuyan! Get that lizard." Copper eyes crackled like sparklers, tails switched purposefully, and their faces arranged in leering devilish grimaces.

During daylight hours the lizards stayed close to the ceiling. They darted from behind curtains or pictures to nip a tasty fly, then scurried back to safety. At night they became more venturesome, to their regret and ours. We probably had more tailless lizards per capita than any other house in Delhi. And lizard corpses were dragged to our bedroom still twitching

<

Sundari on her Everest. Davis

cataleptically so the victor could proudly display his war trophies. If he couldn't waken us with Tarzan howls, he left the cold remains beside the bed for us to step on in the mornings. Thus he left us proof positive of his hunting skills.

One gentle little lizard took up residence behind the light bracket over the living room couch. He was a shy creature and only popped out to catch a chance mosquito; in fact, he owed his longevity to his reclusive routine. Baby Cat and Nuyan eyed him longingly. Sundari regarded their sudden animation with considerable admiration. Like reckless mountaineers, the Persians flung themselves at the sheer precipice of wall, careless of the odds.

On the theory that anything they could do she could do better, Sundari tried her luck. She missed the elusive lizard, but she did latch onto the light fixture. There she dangled like a mobile. In fact, she had so much fun swinging on the brackets that she forgot the original purpose of the game. After that, those who sat under the wall lights—and it was difficult not to—had to be prepared to find Sundari hurtling past their heads at any minute. Even at the expense of loose electric connections, however, I wouldn't make her stop. She looked so ridiculous swinging high above our heads like a spotted chimpanzee, eyes round and grinning with pride in herself. She seemed to be yelling, "Whoopee!"

The cub was nine months old; she had been with us eight months and one week. We had watched her change from cuddly babyhood to gawky adolescence to miniature adulthood. Heretofore we had seen brief glimpses of beauty. Now the grace of her forebears showed in every sleek line of her long powerful body. We were within a month of the absolute time limit set for us and beginning the fourth of limbo. Instead of showing signs of restiveness she was adapting to our new demands—demands which should have been made months before. In three weeks, she had learned to accept the harness and tether and was walking well with us on the barsati and in the house. But the really hard part was yet to come. Sundari would have to emerge into city life. I knew the success or failure of the venture depended solely upon her confidence in me.

The next phase of training was to urge the Cat to come downstairs to the lower landing between the first and second floors. She was fearful and stubborn, so a lot of coaxing and silent swearing went into the effort. But then we got the idea to have her leashed when the school bus was due. Anxious to meet the children, when she heard their voices Sundari agreed to go as far as the door. After that we found it easy to take her to the door at any time. When she found no one saw her in the hallway, she began to enjoy sitting by the door and looking out. The view was uninspiring—a low brick wall topped by a moldering hedge. But through the patchy branches Sundari could watch India pass. Next we propped open the screen door. We were no closer to the street, but one more barrier was down. I sat in the doorway, one arm draped over her shoulders, while Sundari crowded as close as she could.

Hesitant as she was, the leopard was fascinated by the scene. Horse-drawn tongas, their unoiled wheels squealing, rolled by. Massive water buffalo tugged at overloaded carts; their owners whipped hunched shoulders and the metal-shod hooves struck sparks on the pavement. Stray cows searched for edibles—oily rags or discarded rubber flip-flops. Village men in snowy dhotis carried the family suitcase on their heads. Women trailed behind, weighted with children in arms and toddlers clinging to their saris. Elegantly turbaned old gentlemen, beards immaculately laundered, sported walking canes and proudly led grandchildren by the hand. Other children—some completely nude—scrounged for treasures in the street litter. When something particularly interesting caught her fancy, Sundari patted my leg and "ulped" to be sure I didn't miss it. And when I proved that I'd seen it, my reward was a solid buss on the cheek.

It was ten days before Sundari ventured past the open door. I continued to sit in the doorway, but the ten-foot chain let her meander in and out, snuffling and patting unfamiliar territory. The postbox she opened by standing on hind legs. The doorknob on the front door, she found, worked like the others she knew. She examined the stool used by the chowkidaar, or night watchman. She toyed with the dusty red and

143

yellow cannas that leaned against the wall. As her confidence increased, I moved to the chowkidaar stool to let her go farther afield. Daily she became bolder, but still she shied at any unexpected sound, sometimes plunging inside.

We encouraged her to investigate, urged her to go farther from the safety of the house, but we never made any forceful demands. Sundari had to want to take the next step. This approach meant working with the Cat for long hours, much of the time sitting quietly, speaking gently, patting her and praising her when she showed special daring.

In a sense, our hours of work brought Sundari closer than ever to me. Heretofore she had stayed beside me most of the time because she wished to, but she had been free to pursue her own interests as she pleased. It was amusing to imagine how passersby would react if they had known a leopard was scrutinizing their movements. More than ever, it brought home an awareness of Sundari's complete dependence on us. She knew we were there to protect her, but now I was deliberately leading her toward the public—to the very dangers I had avoided.

There was a difference, though. In our home the Cat lived as an equal member of the family, sharing our fortunes and misfortunes, and loved by all of us. She didn't have to face a leering mass of humanity, then return to a lonely cell. Instead, after our sessions, she went upstairs to share her meals with the cats, to launder her people, to tease her servants and accept the applause she deserved. The affectionate support she received made possible her progress.

Inch by inch, step by step, Sundari ventured farther from the door, but always with the knowledge that she could dash back inside. Inevitably, her appearance at the wrought-iron gates drew strangers to peer at us. Just as predictably, when they came near, she lunged for cover. One day as we stood looking through iron curlicues, a man with a small child roared up on a motor scooter. Just as noisily he halted, and when Sundari bolted indoors he shouted, "Come back here! I have brought this girl to see that panther!"

Odd behavior was the order of the day when strangers

144

saw Sundari. Because our leopard was something out of the ordinary, many people felt it their right to crowd close and gape. If they spoke English, they wanted to educate us with all their personal information on "panthers." If not, they felt themselves at liberty to unlatch our gate and intrude into the compound. As the Cat struggled to get away, the chain would bite deeply into my palm. Not seeing the animal's terror or my pain, they would continue to press forward. Finally I began to stage whisper, "Sundari! *Aap-kaa khanna vāahāa hai*—there's your dinner!"

The message was not lost on them; no one seemed to notice the incongruity of one human being pointing out another as a prospective meal. Time and again, I had to tell myself that Sundari and I had to learn to cope with India's illiterate masses; we could no longer remain isolated in the house. Sending my first child off to school was by no means as wrenching an experience as forcing my leopard to accept a life she could not avoid.

By telepathy or grapevine the word spread: there is a cheetah, a *Baagh*—tiger, panther, or whatever—at 10 Nizam-ud-Din East! A babbling stream of curious began ringing our doorbell expecting us to produce the cub for their pleasure at any hour. At first, we politely explained that we could not show her to strangers. Later my refusals became sharper: the zoo was just around the corner. There was no reason to force an unwanted encounter on Sundari within her home. So the grapevine carried a new message and the curiosity-seekers stopped coming so frequently.

On the other hand, our neighbors were kind, and their interest genuine. They kept a safe distance and were happy to speak to us through the gates. But their generosity and their obvious delight in seeing us with the leopard more than balanced the account. It didn't occur to them to think ill of Sundari; they knew better. And without even knowing it, they helped her grow more comfortable with strangers. She was never at ease when a mob gathered, but she soon learned to sit placidly while we talked to the Chopras, the Annands, and the Singhs. Many had called after the disastrous police episode to say how sorry they were, that the world was wrong and Sundari right.

The neighbors were fiercely loyal. If a strange face peered over the hedge or through the gates, women came running from their gardens to shoo the intruder away. Dear, gentle Mr. Chopra, the quiet little rose-gardener, raised his voice to shout, "Begone!" Joe Annand, educated in Sweden, swore in Teutonic English, and the Singhs, good Sikhs to the core, used gentle but persistent persuasion to make their brethren leave.

But even with the neighbors' help, we soon found that Sundari was far more comfortable walking at night. Instinctively she knew that her dappled coat made her nearly invisible, yet her eyesight was unimpaired by the dark. So the children began taking her out, and when they called, "Sundari? Want to go?" she raced to the door. It became a nightly ritual for the youngsters to take her walking. If anything she was more secure with them beside her. Perhaps she thought those of her own age bracket were more understanding.

Six weeks after we had first strapped her into the harness, Sundari was willing to go beyond the gates—very late at night and with all her human props beside her. We never attempted to take her more than a few steps from the gates during the day, and even those expeditions came much later. As with every step we asked but never demanded. When the gates were opened to her, she chose both the moment and the distance. No toddler ever received more praise for taking his first step than Sundari for her first venture through the gate. Never were relatives prouder of a youngster.

Soon she ventured half a block up the street, hugging the shadows of the garden walls all the way, to the entrance of the Moslem tomb maidan. By mid-March, Delhi days are hot, but the nights are still comfortably cool; so that in the meadow, protected by tall hedgerows, Sundari could roll in the pungent, dewy grass and search under bushes for field mice—natural pleasures previously denied her. In the early evening, these grounds were crowded by elderly couples and small groups of teen-agers enjoying the evening respite. But by ten thirty the lawns were nearly empty, and the people who passed through were usually taking a shortcut to the main road.

146

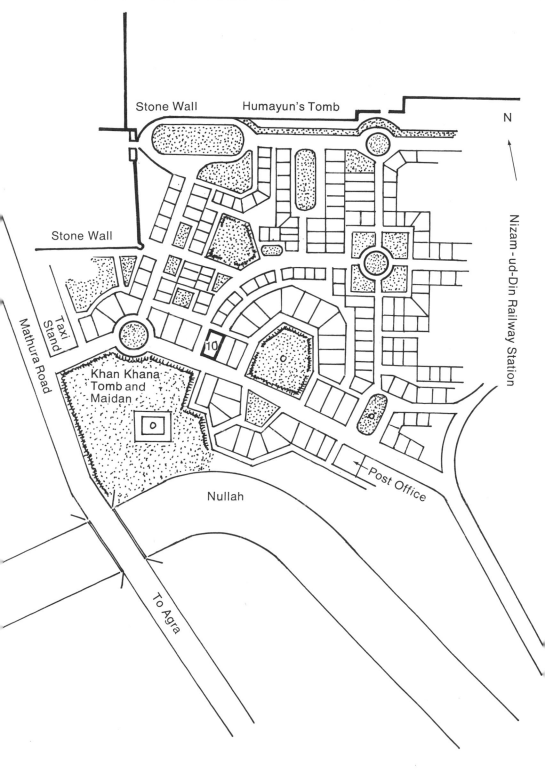

Nizam-ud-Din East. Number 10 was our house.

Each evening Sundari made her inspection tour to be sure nothing had changed during the day. If a moist nose surprised a sleepy chipmunk into angry chatter, all of us fell back in mock surprise. We stalked tall canna blossoms and low stone benches, and we splashed through irrigation puddles. One of us tested the strength of tree bark with her blunted claws and tasted the unpalatable blossoms of pink vinca. The rest of us discovered that forty pounds of leopard can flatten herself out undetectable in six inches of grass, for Sundari did just that whenever people passed. If they noted an animal in the darkness, they simply thought it was a dog—though a sign on the turnstile sternly read, "No Dogs Allowed."

While the youngsters wore the edge off Sundari's energy galloping across the field, I sat cross-legged on the grass smoking, sipping at a communal Coke, and watching my family gambol in the moonlight. Every so often they bore down on my resting spot. Breathlessly they would ask, "Mom, did you see . . .?" Then they passed the Coke around and giggled at Sundari's grimace when she sipped bubbles from cupped hands.

Often, others joined us—Mike Rissler, a PCV, or some friends of the girls spending the night. Young people unused to Sundari were standoffish at first but soon joined in with gusto. They shouted with laughter as she bowled them over, or they tried to catch her unawares. She played with the silly abandon of a huge kitten, and the visitors seemed quite unaware of her wild heritage.

An hour's strenuous romping never did more than blunt the edge of Sundari's vitality, but when the teen-agers grew tired, they allowed her to stalk me. She would move in a series of bounding dashes and flopping halts, then finally leap onto my lap. Of course, she knocked me over and we rolled in the grass. My skirt would be muddied by her paws and my hairdo disheveled beyond hope. More often than not, there'd be new business for the tailor in the morning, but we'd walk home happy and relaxed . . . wondering what we'd ever done to deserve the incomparable experience we were privileged to share.

148

10

AS SUNDARI grew into adulthood, we relied more on Rob as a leopard-sitter whenever I had to be out of the house. We had two reasons. First, we could no longer trust the judgment of our Indian servants. Second, we had a steady flow of delivery men, beggars, salesmen, repair men, and curiosity-seekers at our door. We knew Sundari's only desire was to avoid swarthy-skinned strangers, but we couldn't be sure when some opportunist might decide to force an issue.

In addition, the growing leopard—when left to entertain herself—had taken to barreling through the apartment like a derelict steamroller. Bob had insisted that we hold back our snickers and frown more on her bad behavior. In my shadow, she acted the demure lady, but in my absence she knew that no one else, with the possible exception of Rob, would attempt to control her.

Furniture damage had become a major problem. She had

completely used up the green armchair, so she had turned her attention to the yellow one. Already it looked as though Okies had picked it up secondhand in Death Valley. Unintentionally, her tail was forever whacking sleeping cats, open Cokes, heaped ash trays, leftover sandwiches, and stray teen-agers.

A couple of times, when Rob also had to go out, I returned to find the apartment looking like an earthquake disaster. So I decided that Sundari's activities would at last have to be curtailed. We hated to use the extra bathroom because it had proven so useful as a fifteen-minute delinquent detention center. Yet there Sundari could do less damage. A bathroom it had to be, for there she could not get the running start needed to bank-shoot herself off the walls.

The first time I left her there, she sat in the window looking down as I walked to the car. As the car backed out I could hear her barking, "Come back!"

Feeling a complete heel for leaving her like a bleating lamb, I hurried to finish my errands. Sundari had perhaps an hour to invent a reprisal. On the stairs I could hear a gurgling that sounded like Niagara Falls. Sundari was huddled sopping and trembling on the window sill while steaming, scalding water cascaded from the shower head. She had knocked the fitting askew so that a flood was flowing under doors and into the dining room and our bedroom. While I rubbed down the momentarily penitent Cat, Murli mopped up the floors. We had learned another leopard lesson: we would have to turn off the water under the tub so she couldn't pull that trick again. But we'd have to remember to turn it back on in the evenings. I could just hear Bob's comment if he got into the tub and had no water.

In succeeding days our undaunted demolition expert wrecked the bathroom. She broke the glass shelf over the sink, and loosened the washbowl from its moorings in the wall. The shower-curtain rod came tumbling down. She cracked the top of the toilet tank and brought a list to the wall cabinet. But in that bathroom she had to stay because another problem had developed.

At least one servant was numbly terrified of Sundari—

the mali, or gardener. Twice each day he climbed the steps to the barsati to sprinkle water on those plants he deemed worthy of his attention. He was a little dark brown gnome with a vacant expression and a flapping dhoti. Sundari usually waited for him, concealed under a portulaca. Her game of tease-the-mali began innocently enough when she used tug-the-hose for openers, but then she progressed to yank-the-mali's-dhoti-off. At that point his "AAAAAAAAAAHHHHHHHHHHHs" had the bubbling urgency of a water-logged piccolo.

Unlike Murli, Hari, and Fuzzle, the mali's mind balked at "leopard." Acquainted with her in her infancy, he had even then been fully as afraid as the others were proud of her. My sympathy died with the flowers he tended, and in the end we fired the mali before Sundari could do more than undiaper him. With the mali gone, the heavier gardening chores fell to Rob. Though no great shakes at them, he at least brought verve to the flower pots.

One afternoon while Sundari and I supervised, Rob was mixing manure and sand into the big pile of potting soil that doubled as the barsati cat-box. It was a dusty, unpleasant job. Rob shook his head, pointed to the manure, and solemnly inquired, "Mom? Can you just tell me why Dad has to go buy that stuff when he's already got three cats working at it full time?"

Throughout the spring, as she approached her first birthday, Sundari continued to cut new teeth. Her milk incisors were replaced by gleaming white fangs; the tiny front teeth were gone and in their stead had grown an even row of adult dentition. The front of her mouth looked normal again, but as I examined her mouth, I saw that every molar in her head had been damaged. The discovery rekindled my anger over her mistreatment. Why? Why could anyone fail to see what a beautiful creature she was? Despite her strength, what a rare and fragile animal we had!

Taking her outside the compound strengthened my protective attitude. Our nightly workouts in the maidan were making Sundari as much at home there as in our apartment. She assumed it was her territory and ceased to flatten herself

151

in the grass when strangers passed. Indeed she swaggered down the paths like a maharani strolling with her retainers. On rare occasions when we stopped to chat with friends or neighbors, she sat down, pretending to be a patient household pet. Casual passersby, unknown to us, never guessed that when her swagger switched to swaying undulations, we recognized a mischievous danger signal and shortened her leash.

Her memory amazed and amused us. She remembered the exact bush where a chipmunk had shrilled at us, and she knew the homes of several ground squirrels. She would spend long minutes at each spot trying to rouse the little animals. Once she sat down in front of a little hole—and then leaped into the air unnerved as a chittering squirrel skittered out from under her. Sundari never sat there again, but she spent hours looking for the tiny rodent that had unwittingly bested her.

Dogs reacted in one of two ways—they would slink off whimpering or they would back off yapping. Either way, Sundari remembered the encounters. She carefully investigated places where she had met cowards, and shunned the territory of aggressive dogs. Cattle we always avoided because I'm afraid of them myself.

With her increased assurance, we began walking to other maidans nearby. The other parks in Nizam-ud-Din were smaller and not so well lighted, so that we couldn't race in them, but they did provide a change of scenery and encouraged the Cat to explore new areas. With her late evening walks through our neighborhood, Sundari was at last getting some of the exercise she needed, and her behavior at home improved.

Since we were actually walking the residential streets with her—not just dashing around the grounds of the old tomb—the local police patrols grew accustomed to us. They greeted us pleasantly and didn't seem to think there was anything unusual about a leopard and her entourage prowling Nizam-ud-Din East at odd hours. Friends of Jan and Kris thought it quite an exhilarating experience to ramble with Sundari in the very wee hours, and on one such night they met a police patrol.

"Young ladies, it is not safe for you to be out on the streets

at this hour," said one officer. "You must be going home."
Proper children that they were, they thanked the constables
with straight faces and followed the advice. Later they dis-
solved into peals of laughter. "Think of any poor mugger," they
grinned, "when he'd see Sundari!"

The Cat's self-confidence reached such proportions that
the boys began taking her to sit under the corner neem tree to
watch passersby. She had enjoyed that pastime from the safety
of the front porch and now went willingly with them to the
street in the early evening. The tree was close enough to the
gate that she could bolt home if she wanted. In the shadows
she would sit quietly "ulping" now and then to Rod and Rob,
one on either side of her. Cyclists interested her more than
the foot traffic, perhaps because they moved faster. She pointed
each one out to the boys. One evening they crawled back up
the stairs convulsed with laughter and patting Sundari.

"What a terrific joke!" they whooped. "Mom, she leaped
right smack in front of a guy pedalling along!" The strange
cyclist, seeing Sundari in full lamplight, must have thought
that Kali Durga, goddess of evil, had suddenly dropped from
the night sky to confront him. He had toppled off his stalled
bike, had instantly grabbed it up, and had run down the street,
dragging the vehicle behind.

Sundari was rarely sulky or obstinate, but like all cats, she
had her moments of defiance. Clamping her tongue between
her teeth she would splutter like a naughty child. Once when
she was being particularly impudent and looking sillier for it,
I snatched the tip of her tongue, and waggling it laughed, "I'm
gonna catch a leopard!"

For once in her life Sundari was nonplussed. Her usually
soft-lidded eyes flew wide open. Her whiskers sagged in disbelief. Who would dare to interrupt a leopard in the midst of
her tirade? What's more, sit there and laugh about it?

When she recovered from the shock, she decided the
whole thing had been pretty funny. Thereafter, whether or
not she was moody, I could bend over her with those same
words, and that broad pink tongue would shoot out to be
caught. She never tired of the farce. Though an accidental in-

vention, catch-the-leopard proved a useful game. Sundari was a good-sized handful of cat. When she was dissatisfied or in danger of becoming moody, it was easier to change the direction of her thoughts by a game than by direct discipline. That way she never felt resentment.

March progressed into the oppressive summer heat of April. Bob and I were happy with our family together, but we knew it couldn't last. And in the middle of April, Rob's summons for military duty came.

"Don't make any other plans for April 28," Bob told the girls. "Mom and I want to make his last night home a big family party. I've made reservations at the Chinois."

On that evening, all of us had to dress at the same time. To keep Sundari from joining us in the tubs and splattering our finery, we shut her in the stairwell. We hoped she could gallop off some of her excess energy.

We were nearly ready to go when I heard Bob open the door of the stairwell to call the boys.

"Let's get going!" he yelled. "I'm hungry." Then came a sickening crash and I heard Bob cry out. It was a sound I'd never heard before—Bob howling in sudden pain. I felt a chill.

I ran to the stairwell, and there stood Bob, clutching his right wrist. His index finger was twisted crazily, thrusting obliquely from his hand. Through gritted teeth he said only, "It's broken."

Next to the wall, cowed into a guilty heap, crouched Sundari. So this, I thought, this is the moment we've been warned about.

I dashed for the phone and called the embassy physician, Dr. Carl Nydell. He wasn't in but his wife, Betty, offered help.

"Sundari just attacked Bob!" I cried. "She broke his right index finger."

"Go straight to Holy Family Hospital," Betty said, "and I'll have a surgeon meet you there."

Betty was as good as her word. Better, in fact, for she herself showed up while Bob's finger was being set.

"I decided," said Betty, "if Sundari has turned on the family you'd need somebody here, too."

154

Betty was right. I had been afraid to ask Bob any details. Now the future seemed suspended. Rob was leaving for the Marine Corps, and Sundari—what chance would I have to keep her?

Bob had put up with so much, and I wished miserably it had been my hand rather than his. This had been a terribly painful accident—fortunately not a fatal one—but would the next one be more serious? And might it not happen to one of the children? Such thoughts led to one conclusion: it was my fault for bringing Sundari into our lives.

Even with a mental list of all her faults—and my own— I was terrified that Bob would insist on getting rid of Sundari. It was selfish in the light of all common sense, but I didn't want to give her up.

Bob emerged with a heavily bandaged hand. "I've had pain-killers and a tranquilizer," he said, "but what I'd like is a good martini. Let's go home and get one."

On the way back home to get the youngsters, I finally asked, "How did it happen?"

"I just opened the door to the stairwell," said Bob, "and I guess Sundari decided she'd been in there long enough. I grabbed her neck strap and yanked her back. Well, you know that strap was weak and how slippery the floor is. The Cat jerked back and lost her balance. When she slipped on the stairs, the strap broke and twisted around my finger—crack!"

"You mean"—I was afraid to say it—"Sundari didn't attack you?"

"*Attack* me?" Bob roared. "Hell, no. You know better than that. It wasn't the Cat's fault!"

Driving through Delhi traffic I could have cried in sheer relief. In fact, I did. In spite of fright and rough handling, Sundari hadn't overreacted.

And so for Rob's farewell dinner we managed a measure of festivity. Though he was uncomfortable and awkward, Bob was in fine form, gesturing with his bandage like a young Sundari. He grinned at the children, "You know, don't you, this could have happened with any animal your mother might have chosen? Cape buffalo, python, wild boar, or elephant . . ."

The next morning early, after we got home from seeing Rob off, Sundari made her morning rounds. She went to Rob's bed first, then looked for him in the boys' bath. She greeted Rod and went to 'say good morning to the girls. She didn't waste much time with them and didn't stop to get her breakfast—the first time she had willingly postponed a meal. Returning to the barsati bedroom, the Cat checked every place Rob had ever hidden in their games of hide-and-seek—under the bed, on top of the almirah, behind the shower curtain. Not finding him, she climbed into his bed and looked among his covers. Then she did an astonishing thing. She began wallowing among those covers, whimpering. And finally she gave the bark that meant, "Come here!"

We left Rob's spread unchanged and unwashed to see how long Sundari would continue to look for him. I knew she couldn't scent him, but that she knew where he should be; if she looked long enough and hard enough she thought she would find him. Even when Rod had also gone away to attend college, and their beds were moved to a downstairs bedroom, Sundari found Rob's old bed and went there each morning to call her pal. She kept to her search for the next ten months, seeking the boy that she loved and missed.

Summer's increasing heat forced us to walk Sundari later and later in the evenings. Many residents of Delhi spend long evenings in the maidans to catch a light breeze. Premonsoon heat has a blast furnace quality; even the air from rotating electric fans seems hot and searing. The poor get what relief they can wherever they find it; some even spread sheets on the grass of the parks to spend the night.

Since Sundari was uneasy surrounded by strangers, we had to wait until eleven thirty or later to take her out on especially torrid evenings. I soon learned to take a nap first, setting the alarm for midnight. Kris was always ready to go with us, and Jan came along if we could rouse her long enough to get herself dressed. Occasionally, when I was too tired to go, Kris took the Cat alone. Kristy's judgment and ability to handle Sundari were second only to Rob's, and Sundari showed that she valued our sixteen-year-old daughter's companionship.

156

There is something about strolling the streets of a huge city at night with a great cat. The experience isolates a person from the rest of humanity. But it isn't a lonely isolation. It gives one a quiet sense of elation; the world is not so much shut out as unable to intrude. No one else may know or care that you are there—but *you* know. You and those with you are a closed society neither needing nor wanting other companionship. While the world sleeps you are awake.

Not quite all the world sleeps at night, we found. And thus we met the chowkidaars of Delhi.

Chowkidaars are a custom peculiar to India. Placing little faith in their constabulary, suspicious by nature, and preoccupied with thievery, Indians not only padlock and nail down all movable objects, they also hire watchmen by the house and the block. On the surface the practice seems a sensible precaution except for two details.

First, it is commonly accepted that many house robberies occur with the connivance—or the collaboration—of chowkidaars. We ourselves never suffered a burglary. All the right people had met Sundari *à la belle étoile,* knew where she lived, and preferred not to test wits with her at home *à la dérobée.*

The second point is that chowkidaars are uncompromising in their demands for a night's rest. They will go to any lengths to get it. As a staff of office, the chowkidaar carries a stout straight shillelagh which he thumps on the ground with every step. Those who are paying his salary cannot sleep—nor can anyone else nearby—with the pounding racket, and are well aware that their servant is on the job. Thus kept awake till midnight, the employer finally falls into exhausted sleep—and then so does the chowkidaar.

For a time AID—the Agency for International Development—supplied house guards for us. Of the many who dozed by our portals, I recall one overzealous individual who gave a resounding clout to each of the ground floor air-conditioners as he passed. The noise was terrible. Until he slept, we could not.

When AID, in an economy move, decided to dispense with the services of guards, we heaved a sigh of relief. But

Bud Rissler, our groundfloor neighbor, suggested that it might be a good thing if we went halves on a replacement. Bob's simple reply was, "Okay. Any time you want to foot half Sundari's food bill it's fine with me."

On our nightly excursions, we met the Nizam-ud-Din East chowkidaars just where we expected to find them: under shrubs, wedged among low branches, propped against gateposts, stretched corpselike on stone benches. One night we found a chowkidaar sleeping soundly on a raised traffic island in the middle of the street. Perversely, Sundari decided that night watchmen should be awake and watchful. She leaped right in front of him. He awoke, saw, and shrieked—though his cry faded as he disappeared down the street. He left behind his turban and baton.

One midnight as we walked on the edge of the tomb maidan in moonlight bright as noontime, a chowkidaar rolled off his charpoy beside the tomb and started toward us across the green. He must have been new and unfamiliar with our story, for he seemed bent on evicting a trespassing dog and its owners. I called to him, "*Piichii jaaoo*—go back," but he ignored the warning.

Then Sundari landed in front of him. She was only teasing, but the man couldn't be expected to know that. With an earsplitting howl, he took off through spurting gravel. He must have set up his bed on the other side of the tomb after that, for we never saw him again.

Chowkidaars, interesting diversions though. they were, didn't absorb all our walking time. Delhi streets seem deserted at night only by comparison with the day. During work hours, one picks a way through sugarcane hand presses, sidewalk shoe-repair shops, beggars, parked cars, sadhus, brick piles, pye-dogs, bicycle-repair stands, barbers, cigarette peddlers, and unclaimed cows. All that commerce stays on the walkway. On the street itself, one dodges a welter of honking trucks, bellowing buffalo, stalled buses, goat herds, shambling oxcarts, impatient taxis, speeding scooters, wavering cycles, horse tongas, and itinerant pedestrians. Delhi is truly the world's largest village.

158

At night the vendors are gone, along with the sidewalk repair shops. The beggars snore under hedges, and the sadhus have returned to their holy places. The rampant flood of buses, trucks, and humanity recedes, but it never dries up. The traffic tide from Nizam-ud-Din Railway Station still ebbs and flows, and the tank truck of the Delhi Milk Scheme zooms down the side streets to make deliveries. A local bull and his harem graze on one maidan and then another. From Mathura Road comes the minor-key melody of vehicular traffic.

At two o'clock in the morning, one hears the petulant whine of sick children, dogs barking, a train rumbling toward the station with whistle awail. From the servants' quarters behind a bungalow comes the angry buzz of voices raised in argument. Irrigation water gurgles in the maidans and millions of insects drone over damp grass. Down by the corner at the taxi stand the clarion clang of steel on steel announces that one enterprising driver is beating his engine into submission. Jackals yelp in the nullah, and next door two caterwauling tomcats get down to their disagreement. Somewhere in the distance a temple loudspeaker squawks religious music. Nearer, in the colony of mud huts by the railroad, the primitive throb of bass drums beats out a tribal rhythm. Here the lonely hoot of an owl; there the screech of a hungry hawk. The soft slap-slap of bare feet and the clatter of shod hooves on pavement tell a story of India: an animal with shoes and a man without. Roman candles, adjuncts of Hindu weddings, bloom in the night sky and explode over the chug-chug of a two-cylinder scooter rickshaw. This is the din of overcrowded and overburdened humanity, the song of India's pathos. And in the light of day it is amplified a thousandfold.

From Rob came brief letters; he was in Marine Corps boot camp. He missed us all, especially the Cat. With our son gone, Sundari had to spend more and more time shut up in the bathroom; I simply had too many chores outside the house. If she was to remain a full-fledged member of the family, I realized she would have to learn to ride in the car. We approached this training course as we had others in the Cat's

159

education. First we encouraged her to clamber over the outside of the car; she did so willingly. Open doors next invited her to inspect the inside without feeling cramped or trapped. This phase, though gradual, moved faster than our lessons to get her out of doors. When she had nosed the steering wheel, slapped the spare tire, jiggled the turn signals, and turned down the sun visors, we shut the doors and started the engine. She couldn't have cared less when we slowly moved forward and then backward ten feet.

We thought her sufficiently at ease in ten days to take a trial spin. We chose six o'clock in the evening as the best time for the test. At that hour in Delhi the tempo of afternoon activities has slowed down, but the evening homeward rush has not begun. Housewives are inside preparing the evening curry. Tea stalls are nearly deserted, and it is still too hot for many children to be playing in the maidans. It is light, but the low sun casts long gray-purple shadows.

Our first drives were of short duration and confined to neighborhood streets that Sundari knew well. At first she snuggled close to me, keeping a paw and most of her weight on my thigh. We necessarily rode in low gear because in our gear-shift car I couldn't lift my foot from the accelerator to the clutch. Sundari was subdued, a new pose for her, but new sights had always intrigued her; if these were not unfamiliar, at least she was seeing them in a new light.

I felt like a test pilot who had broken the sound barrier. Sundari realized she was safe in the car, and she wasn't flinching from people she saw; she was watching them with ears forward and whiskers at right angles, a sure sign of enjoyment.

Soon Sundari was riding with me to transport our youngsters to visit friends or to the swimming pool—five miles from home. She always had a group of admiring teen-agers waiting to speak to her. But half an hour of Delhi streets was long enough for the Cat. After that she became restless.

By daylight in the car, people could see her—and take notice. Curiously enough, we actually added to the confusion of the byways of Delhi. One scooter driver, gazing at us, plowed into a tree. Cars pulled abreast with driver and passengers alike hanging from the windows to howl questions at us. At least one truck-taxi accident could be laid to us because both drivers were so busy gaping that they crashed head-on.

If we pointed out herds of goats or cattle to Sundari, she firmly turned her back on them—she refused to look. We wondered whether she was afraid of so many, though she didn't act it, or whether she just couldn't count above two. But when she saw one or two animals together she took great interest.

Horses were Sundari's favorites. Whenever she saw one, she "ulped" and patted us to be sure we saw, too. Her whiskers tilted up and her lips drew back in that smile peculiar to felines. Perhaps the horses moved with more style than other animals, though most Indian ponies are scrawny, stunted, galled, and infested with botflies.

In June, two days before Sundari's first birthday, Rod left for the United States to attend college. Sundari looked for him in his bed, but she didn't cry for him as she still did for Rob. Rod had taken over almost completely the chore of galloping the leopard in the maidan; she was certainly fond of him and missed him, but her heartache was for Rob.

And then Sundari was one year old. She weighed nearly sixty long sleek pounds. She had become a bond uniting the family at a time when youngsters begin trying their wings. She had adjusted to the comforts of home with little effort and no regrets for the paths of nature, but what was she? A leopard who thought she was a person, or a person in leopard spots? We didn't know. We only knew we were two months past the absolute time limit set for us—and that we still had no intention of giving her up.

However, for whatever reason, if you choose to live with an animal that society dreads, then you must be prepared to face repercussions. Sundari's unique position in a city of three and a half millions set us apart. Even small cats are unpopular

First birthday portrait, on June 9, 1968. Davis.

One year old, June 9, 1968. This is Jan's favorite photograph of the leopard and one of the family favorites. The author is particularly fond of it because the Cat is so obviously confident, relaxed, and satisfied. Would you be afraid of such a benign animal?
Charlotte Bush

in India. Hindu fear and dislike of cats is exemplified by Kali Durga, goddess of evil and destruction, who rides a tiger. The tiger is Kali's symbol.

Aware of the Indian attitude toward felines, I knew that as soon as we began taking Sundari out of the compound we were opening the door to complaint. In June the protest came.

One morning, right after Bob had gone to work, the phone rang.

"I am a neighbor," shouted a much agitated male voice on the line. "No, no. I will not identify myself! You are endangering the whole community! You have no regard for others. You Americans think you can get away with anything! Well, I shall put an end to your arrogance!"

He continued to shout, often irrationally. On one point he was entirely mistaken: we depended completely on the goodwill of our neighbors and friends.

In the first minutes of his harangue, a numbing fear seeped through me. Then I grew angry.

The anonymous man raged on. He and his infant grandson, he said, had seen us talking to another American the previous evening. The child had immediately become terrified. The child had cried all night and was now afraid to go into the garden because of the voracious beast at large. He finished his comments shouting, "Now I demand—demand!—that you give me the telephone number of your husband." I gave it to him since he could easily have obtained it from the embassy. His parting shot was, "Mr. Davis may be more reasonable!"

I thought perhaps he had a point there. Bob's finger was just out of the cast, and it still pained him constantly. For an hour I cradled Sundari's head in my lap while I worked up the nerve to check with Bob. When I finally called him, Bob asked, "What did you two do last night? Pull the wrong stunt on the right person?"

"No, not last night," I said. "We didn't even see anybody."

Convinced that we had not, for once, created a disturbance, Bob outlined a plan of action for me. First, I called the only person we had seen the night before; on our friend's suggestion I notified the security section of the embassy that we had had an unpleasant encounter with an Indian national. To my vast relief, the security chief told me not to worry; his office would take no action against us unless they had concrete proof that the leopard was a menace. In his opinion, the man was merely blowing off steam and would not bother us again. But if he did we were to refer the anonymous caller to that office.

That night as Bob and I compared notes, we saw that our caller really was a crank. My anonymous caller had identified himself to Bob by name—but not as a neighbor. He had threatened to call the police, the district magistrate, the embassy—and if they failed to punish us, he would take his case to the Nizam-ud-Din Citizens' Association.

No one bluffs Bob. All his replies were reasonable; for example: "The police have been acquainted with Sundari for several months." Nothing more.

"My wife has a court order remanding the leopard to her custody."

"If you wish to call the embassy the number is 70351."

And finally, "Unless citizen associations are more influential here than are those of my country, I don't think it will do you much good."

But we weren't reassured by the knowledge that our caller was a crank. He could be harmful. For the moment we were safe, but still I felt we must have some sort of reserve plan for Sundari's safety. Bob thought differently. "Forget it!" he said. "You won't hear from that guy again."

I didn't suppose we would. I was still so concerned, though, that I called Mr. Sankhala for advice. "Why don't you bring Sundari to walk in my garden?" he suggested. "When she feels secure, she will be my child. We will introduce her into the zoo gradually."

I would not consider that solution. No one would treat Sundari as we did, and she could not exist in a home under any other conditions. But walking her in the Sankhala's own garden might help; it certainly couldn't hurt. If we were ever forced to move her in a hurry, at least the surroundings would be familiar to her. And so, very reluctantly, I agreed to take

Sundari to the zoo in late afternoons—back to the place of her beginnings.

Mr. Sankhala's neatly barbered lawn was protected from the street by a high stone wall and a strip of dense undergrowth. Beyond a formal garden and a bougainvillaea hedge stretched a large overgrown meadow. "But don't walk there," Mr. Sankhala warned, "It has cobra lairs."

We were also banned from the strip of jungle beside the wall—more cobras. But the meadow, cobwebbed with straggling foot paths, should have been an excellent isolated spot for walking Sundari. It wasn't. First, the buffalo and goats grazed there. Then, too, dozens of people lived nearby: the families of the zoo director and his deputies, the zoo vet, plus an assortment of uncles, aunts, and kiddies.

And there was Sundari herself. She didn't like walking into new places except under cover of darkness when the shadows blended her coat into invisibility. She didn't appreciate people popping up from clumps of grass or plopping down out of trees in front of her. Both of us shared the suspicion that buffalo masticated with evil intent while they glared at us.

To prove her determination not to be pushed into anything she hadn't thought of herself, Sundari sat down. She wouldn't budge. It just isn't easy to walk a sixty-pound leopard when her rear seems glued to the ground. I went home each day with arms and legs quivering from fatigue, and if Sundari didn't have a sore backside she should have.

After watching our Mutt and Jeff performance for a week, Mr. Sankhala pronounced, "Her behavior is typical of leopards."

I couldn't help wondering irreverently how many he'd seen dragged around on their rumps, but it was no time to pick a quarrel. "Why don't you and your family come to tea tomorrow afternoon?" I asked instead. He hadn't seen Sundari at home for a long time; perhaps he would change his mind about her.

I also hoped Sundari would change hers. Her aversion to

the director manifested itself in the way she hissed softly through clenched teeth.

When they arrived the next afternoon, Sundari was beside me—on the leash where I could ensure her best behavior. It was the first time she had been so restrained in our home, but we couldn't risk a scene.

The Cat had no grudge against Mr. Sankhala or Predeep, who now fed Sundari cheese from his fingers. But when the director attempted the same advance, she nipped at his hand, then turned her backside as though to say, "Not on your tintype! I'll starve first."

During the two hours of their visit, the tip of Sundari's weather-vane tail flicked nervously. Her body, always so sprawlingly relaxed, stretched tense. Her face, usually so gentle, seemed angular with wariness.

As they left, Mr. Sankhala urged me to continue coming to his garden; with time Sundari might change. I knew she wouldn't. It would be pointless to go on. "No, I think not," I answered. "But thank you for trying to help. We'll go on walking where she is happy. If we have another crisis, we'll just have to meet it as best we can."

At least we had increased Sundari's mobility with the motorcar outings. By now she considered the car her own. I stood in high favor because she knew I was the chauffeur. She had given up all pretense of riding quietly by my side and now rode wherever she pleased.

Her favorite perch was just behind the driver where she sat on the seat. Her hind legs and tail dribbled onto the floor while her front paws encased my shoulders. Her chin usually rested comfortably in the curve of my neck. From that advantageous spot she could wash my ears and tickle my neck with her feathery whiskers. She could also issue a commentary on my driving or the scenery, or she could stage love-ins with equal ease.

Invariably, Sundari chose the worst times to shower me with affection. In the middle of intersections, or just as we pulled into the opposite lane to pass a line of traffic, she would rise up and plunk her chest on top of my head to begin the ritual. Her weight forced me down in the seat or forward until my nose rested on the wheel. In either case, it left the driving chore to the Cat. Actually, as Indian drivers go, she was among the best.

Sundari had become very possessive of her seat. She wanted no one to put an arm on the back of the front seat. When they did she gave a warning nip to the usurping elbow or wrist. She didn't aim to hurt—merely to intimidate, for she never broke the skin or left a bruise. She knew exactly how much pressure to exert to get off scot-free.

Her arbitrariness wasn't mean and she never directed it toward the driver. Therefore, I took the Cat along whenever I could. My only alternative was locking her up—which she hated as much as I. In fact, the alternative probably contributed to her relatively pacific behavior in the car.

Yet even on rides she kept some tricks up her speckled sleeve. Once when we picked up Kristy from a party, Kris asked if I would give a new friend of hers a lift home. The girl had just arrived in India, so I murmured an objection on the grounds that Sundari might be obnoxious. Kris, however, insisted, "That's okay, Mom. Everyone knows Sundari!"

That wasn't the point, but I gave in. And that youngster will probably never forget our leopard either. Sundari let the girls settle on the back seat and then plopped herself onto the newcomer's lap. For the next two miles Kristy's friend was subjected to a most thorough feline facial. Heaven knows what she told her parents that night.

The teen-agers who knew Sundari were most understanding. They spoke gently and patted her and were not forward with her—all traits that endeared them to a feline. But the general public remained my great worry. As we paused one day at an intersection, a man actually rammed his fist in the rear window.

In an instant Sundari's whole body slammed toward the offender. Her growl began somewhere under the Bay of Bengal, deep and full of thunder. The window glass was half way up and that alone saved the stranger's arm. He drew back with barely a split second to spare.

The incident unnerved me. It would never occur to the intruder, nor to the authorities, that anyone was at fault save the leopard and her careless owners. We were creating an attractive nuisance. And for the first time I had to face the fact that Sundari would strike to kill if she felt sufficiently threatened.

Any dog might react in the same manner. But that wasn't important. Society recognizes dogs as a natural part of the scene; dogs can bite without a scandal, but not so leopards. A great cat defending its territory is still considered a predator. A man-eater. Regardless of the provocation.

11

THE PEDESTRIAN intruder had warned us well. But clearly we could not drive around in the scorching premonsoon weather with our windows closed. All of us would suffocate. The station wagon had plently of room for Sundari behind the back seat, and safety demanded that bars be installed. In effect, we would be caging my darling, though only for her own protection.

One of the project drivers from Bob's office acted as my translator while I explained our needs to a carpenter. The wooden bars could be removed and folded for storage when necessary. Sundari meantime didn't take kindly to the arrangement. She didn't much mind entering the car through the tailgate, but she had a lot to say about being kept from the middle of her family. So for the first week one of the girls had to sit on the back seat and talk to her while we rode.

With the bars installed, we were far more comfortable in

At fifteen months, behind bars for her own protection. Charlotte Bush

all ways. Sundari was protected from officious intruders and all of us could get some cross ventilation. But even with bars, we still found our Delhi chores unsatisfactory. Parked, we collected hordes of idlers who did anything to make the leopard react. They beat on the car with fists and packages, made weird noises, and plastered their noses against the windows. Sundari obliged them by snarling, laying her ears against her skull, and lashing her tail ominously. Such stupid cruelty enraged me, but I could do nothing to stop the idlers.

While we drove, pedestrians seldom noticed Sundari, and when they did we were far enough away to avoid contact. But we had a good chuckle from some—like the seedy Western flower child who saw us and stood gaping in awe.

"See that hippy," I said, unable to resist moralizing. "We don't have to reject all accepted behavior to do our own thing."

The girls caught the drift of my message, but twisted it a bit. "Now, Mom," they said. "Wouldn't you agree that most of your friends think you're a little 'different'?"

The youngsters had long had their fun with my "differentness." Once at a diplomatic reception, when Bob had been out of town and my sons had escorted me, a visiting dignitary asked me about India's great cats. I began to wax eloquent about Sundari when, from the corner of my eye, I noted some odd gestures. My two sons were silently mouthing, "She hasn't got a leopard" at a spot directly behind my back. Their fingers were describing circles at the side of their heads. When I turned again to look at the visitor, I found him deeply engrossed in our conversation—and prepared to humor me. I've often wondered whether he ever found out that there really was a leopard in our house.

But perhaps there was just a measure of "differentness" in our situation. And even I began to wonder whether the doubters might be right when Sundari suddenly became cranky. She was so nasty that I decided to try giving her raw meat as her first step toward zoo life. If she continued in her present vein, her days at home were numbered. Then the reason dawned: the only period she had been temperamental was the time her teeth hurt.

172

She really didn't want a dental examination, and I used a lot of cheese to convince her. But there lay the answer: Two molars—one broken far down into the gum—had loosened. The irritation was great. Though I found no infection, her mouth was too tender for eating. On top of the other discomfort, she was hungry.

No matter how ill she felt, Sundari wanted to go for her nightly rambles. She especially enjoyed leaping into trees high as the leash allowed. But one night her leap scared out a colony of bats. They exploded from the tree in a noisy rush. Sundari shot back out of the tree and landed running on all fours. Thereafter Sundari was careful to stay out of young royal palms.

Except when there were imperative reasons for haste, we didn't run because when Sundari got started I bobbed along behind like the tail of a kite until she decided to stop. Sometimes she halted so quickly that she catapulted me snappily over her back and onto my own. Each time it happened, though, she sweetly waited until I had picked up my remnants of arms and legs and wits.

Usually Sundari was content to walk sedately by my side. It gave her more opportunity to investigate each shrub and clump of grass for the ground squirrels and little brown rats that abound in India. After monsoon began, instead of waiting until nearly midnight to go out, we had to dash out between showers after nine o'clock, but we still preferred the later hours.

Finally one molar fell out and then the larger part of the second dropped away; now Sundari took a new interest in food. In another few days the last bit of baby tooth was forced out by the new molar and Sundari became her charming self, vain of appearance and boisterous of manner.

I felt less boisterous myself. The monsoon moisture laid me low, so that Bob finally asked, "Why don't you go on up to Mussoorie?"

Mussoorie, a Kumaun hill resort, teeters at six thousand cool feet above sea level among deep pine forests. One of my dearest friends, Ruth Matsuura, spent the summer months there with her six children. Ruth had been urging me to visit her but I had hesitated.

"What would I do with Sundari?" I asked Bob. "I can't leave her."

"Take her with you," said Bob. "Isn't that why you got bars for the car? If you have to, you can put her in the car at night." The idea made good sense. Only one thing gave me pause. Sundari had never been in the car for a prolonged period; on the way we couldn't let her out for nature calls. But the Cat, I decided, would just have to be patient.

Next morning with the luggage on the rack, the Cat tucked into her cage, and the girls on the back seat to keep her company, we started on the 190-mile trek. Over the antiquated Jumna bridge and through Delhi's congested out-skirts, Sundari whined her complaints and paced as much as the confined quarters allowed. But once out into the open country where she could see long stretches of green and beige fields with cattle and buffalo and people, she settled down and rode well. The day was sunny and hot, and when we found isolated spots we stopped to give her water. Because we'd for-gotten to bring a bowl for her, we served her from the lid of our own Thermos. Then we shared our tuna sandwiches, though she turned down the pickles we offered.

As we began ascending the Himalayan foothills, we could see Mussoorie far ahead, clinging to the side of its steep mountain. The air was already cooler and the emerald green of pine-clad hills was a relief after the endless plain. In Mussoorie, I had no idea where to find the house.

"For a small sum you can hire a coolie to take you there," a constable wisely suggested. The coolie, delighted with the prospect of a relaxing ride in an American car, stuck his head in the rear window. A roar knocked it out again. In fearful disbelief, he preferred to trot off ahead of us.

We navigated the station wagon through the defiles of the bazaar. Warping the wide car along constricted chasms, dodging pack-laden coolies, handcarts, and goats, we came to a dead standstill every few feet while cycles, children, and cows were hauled into shops to let us pass the narrow crannies.

174

Finally, the coolie pointed his finger high over our heads to a house perched three hundred feet straight above us and announced, "Suncliff *vāahāa hai*—Suncliff is there."

It was just as well. The girls bolted from the car and looked around.

"Hey, Mom!" said Jan. "Take a look at the mob we've collected!" At least fifty idlers now crowded around, gesticulating and shouting.

The Matsuuras couldn't fail to hear the hullabaloo below, so they came streaming down the path to greet us. From Peter, age eleven, to Andy, age four, little Matsuuras bounced all around shouting and laughing and grabbing parcels. We asked their cook to scatter some of our followers before taking the heavier luggage up to the house. Ruth now appeared saying, "Oh, Rocky! How wonderful!"

Greater love hath no woman than to welcome a house guest with a leopard. But that was Ruth, an extraordinary American with the delicate features of her Japanese ancestry. The wife of a University of Illinois plant breeder, Ruth herself was a psychologist and pediatrician—the only one I've ever met who raised her own practice. Her household was equal to any problems we brought. And they began before we got to the house.

After periodic objections to the long dusty ride, Sundari now said she definitely preferred the car to the human horde outside. We hauled her protesting from the rear. It was like pulling a cork from a bottle. She erupted roaring with outrage—and effectively dispersed most of the crowd. Then Jan and Kris took turns pushing and pulling Sundari uphill.

Again we were making a spectacle of ourselves. And no wonder. These simple mountain people lived in daily dread of great cats. Their enthusiastic folktales magnified the exploits of tigers and leopards to the supernatural. Now they were seeing three apparently deranged American women hoisting a huge leopard up the side of a mountain. For Mussoorie, this was the circus of the century. And they hit the trail behind us to watch.

Ruth had wonderful accommodations for Sundari in a

175

detached guest cottage behind the main house. Sundari had been uprooted and was so sweetly confused over the whole day's proceedings that we wanted to remove her from the hustle-bustle of the big house. Kristy elected to sleep there with us while Jan chose to stay with the little Matsuuras.

Jan cuddled the Cat on her lap while Kris and I made a cat-box from a cardboard carton lined with plastic and filled with leaves and pebbles. The steep mountainside had no sand or dirt. "At least we have some meat," said Ruth. She had brought us the remains of yesterday's mutton roast as a snack. "And I've arranged for the gosht-wallah to come every day." And certainly the meat man would be essential.

But Sundari sniffed at her sandless sandbox and then at the roast. She turned up her nose at both.

I have heard over and over that when large cats are confused and afraid they are the most dangerous. Maybe. The fact remains that Sundari's behavior during our nine-day stay with the Matsuuras could only be described as angelic—all out to prove she was the dearest, gentlest animal on earth, she patted and kissed—and please-don't-leave-her. She greeted the few visitors to whom we allowed interviews with distinguished composure, sitting demurely on the charpoy and smiling shyly with her chin tucked into her chest. She was so genuinely bent on proving her model deportment that I thought her kisses at night were designed to remind me of her irreproachable nature.

Later I decided she simply wanted more room on the single charpoy we shared. Two-thirds of the cot went to the Cat, and I had to curl up like an embryo with my knees in my face.

Knowing it would be impossible to get Sundari to have a bowel movement outside during the day, we took her out at night to walk round and round the house. We couldn't go farther because the house was surrounded by forest. The heavily timbered hillside was too dark for us to see a thing. Sundari might not have impaired vision, but I had no desire to descend the mountain head over teacups and lose the Cat in the bargain.

176

But there was another reason, too. On our first morning there, Peter came up to say, "I saw Sundari getting into the garbage cans last night."

"Oh, no," I said, "She was on the leash when we were out."

"But she was outside running loose," Peter insisted, "and she knocked off the lid of the garbage can."

Ruth overheard us. "Peter," she said, "you don't suppose that was the wild leopard." And then we heard the story. Only a week before, the neighbors had left their Pekingese tethered in the garden overnight. A wild leopard had jumped over their wall, killed the dog, and eaten him on the spot. "And other people here have seen a wild leopard raiding garbage cans," Ruth added. "Apparently a female."

"Neat-o!" said Jan.

"I'd like to see that one!" said Kris.

"Yes," I agreed a bit illogically, "I'd like to see a *real* leopard."

That night we didn't see one, but shortly after we turned out our lights, we clearly heard its paws land on the roof of the guest house. It had bounded down from the steep mountainside behind us, then presumably it leaped off our roof to the ground. We even heard the garbage can rattle, but by the time we got to the door, the creature had made a getaway.

"Next time," said Kris, "we'd better wait up to see it."

A few nights later we did exactly that. First we took Sundari for her garden walk. She still quite refused to rough it and would do no more than urinate on the rocky hillside. Inside again, we secured ourselves, turned off the lights, and waited at the unlatched door. The night air was chill, but both Kris and I stood sphinx-still, hardly daring to breathe.

We hadn't long to wait before the marauder clunked again onto the tin roof. In half a minute Kris threw the door wide open. With a feeling of excitement, I stepped out onto the porch. There below us—not thirty feet away—I could see a shadow move. Here was the camouflage I knew so well, but this time that dappled coat was not ours. At that instant I heard a terrifying sound: the door slammed behind me. I was locked outside with a "real" leopard. My loved ones were nestled snug inside.

There is considerable difference between sleeping with a pet leopard and finding oneself locked outside with a wild one. The irony wasn't lost on me even in my terror. Perhaps I stood there sixty seconds. It seemed like an hour. Panic-stricken, I pounded on the door with clenched fists. "Kris!" I screamed. "Let me in! Let me in!"

She did. Meantime, our own hypocritical roseate impostor usurped a whole charpoy and feigned deep sleep. I got inside quaking, all my desire to see a "real" one entirely gone. No wild leopard would have dallied long with all the racket. But it brought home to me the very real terror some people felt when they saw Sundari. We could, and did, laugh at my hysterical effort to get back into the room. And yet, I had not always accepted the same alarm in others.

With my own bad example to follow, Sundari showed no bravery at all. She preferred to meet no mountain kin and to learn no mountain lore. During our nine-day stay she did not once have a bowel movement. She waited till we began our return journey. Then half a mile down the road, as we entered Mussoorie bazaar, Sundari's physical needs exceeded her fastidiousness. With great embarrassment, she fouled the car.

Our mountain holiday brought us a postscript two weeks after our return to Delhi.

"They finally shot that wild leopard at Three Sisters Bazaar," wrote Ruth. "That's only a block from our house. They found it was a nursing female—a real pity. I told the men to look for cubs. I felt sure you would be willing to keep them until they were placed with a zoo."

Bob listened quietly. "Does she mean a complete litter?" I nodded. "Would you?"

"Well, for a while I would. Maybe two or three months."

But Bob needn't have worried. The cubs were never found.

Things ran smoothly for the next month. For one thing,

Hari had returned to our kitchen, replacing Fuzzle, who had developed an expensive taste for Drambuie. Once more Hari indulged Sundari in all her culinary fancies. We had returned to a tranquil Golden Age.

Sundari herself was less rambunctious in the house, and our nightly roamings were uneventful. It was still hot and muggy and we kept all doors shut so the air-conditioners would operate at peak efficiency.

The morning paper had my attention one morning when Hari yanked open the door. He seemed unable to speak. His jaw worked but he couldn't make a sound. Finally, mute, he turned and threw open the door into the stairwell. But I had already smelled the trouble. Acrid smoke engulfed me.

The fuse boxes and electric meters for the whole house were located on the lower landing of the stairs. Twice before we had small fires there, but this one looked much worse. Black noxious clouds billowed into the hall before we could shut the door.

"Get the girls up. And make them get dressed!" I told Hari, then ran to wet down a towel and cover my face. Thus shielded, I tried to get down the stairs far enough to assess the danger. There was plenty. Smoke and heat forced me back.

The phone was still working, so I called Norma Rissler, downstairs. "We're on fire!" I yelled. "The stairwell is blocked. We'll have to climb down from the barsati. I'll call AID, if you'll try the fire department."

I rang off and told the girls to wait on the barsati with the servants and little cats. Our solid masonry walls weren't going to burn very fast. And on the roof they would be in no danger from smoke inhalation. Our children have spent their lives proving they are related to monkeys; they would have no trouble rappelling down the outside pipes if they had to. I assumed the servants could do the same. They ran up the steps and I slammed the door behind them. I was then unaware that Ram Prashad, our dhobi, was still doing laundry in the godown.

My next step was to call Bob. He could jog the AID maintenance office with greater urgency than I could. In the midst of crisis, I clearly recalled other crises: like the time Sundari pulled some pipes out of the wall and we had water gushing all over the barsati for seven hours before AID got around to us.

Phoning in India is never simple. Aside from the mechanical difficulty, one observes a ritual in reaching the desired party. Bob's office was on the third floor and the telephone clerk was on the first. We therefore practiced all the rites.

I requested Dr. Davis, please.

"Who is this speaking, please?" (This petition had often tempted me to inquire just how many women phone my husband.) Next comes a rundown on the health of each member of the family. After such amenities, the clerk went out for a cup of tea. That was the only explanation for the delay. Ten minutes later he came back. "Dr. Davis is not in," he reported.

"Well, get me any of the Americans in the office, please," I asked. "My house is on fire and we can't get out."

Instead, he got the office manager, another Indian. Just then I heard the pier window in the stairway—a window two stories high—split with the crack of a powerful rifle. Frightened, I shouted, "Get me an American—Mr. Lansing, Dr. Williams—I don't care who, but get one in a hurry!"

That penetrated. Walt Lansing, hastily summoned, came on the line. "I'll call AID," he promised, "and find Bob for you."

The fire was crackling noisily as it licked up the paint. Ebony-oily smoke seeped under the door and made my eyes smart. "We're okay, Mom," Jan called down from the barsati. Even with Walt's reassuring words, I was still worried; but it was too late to get Sundari up the steps to the roof.

I had to get her out of the house somehow. That stairwell was the only exit from our apartment, and until now I had thought what a good idea it was. I was trying to figure out some way when I noticed Ram Prashad standing quietly in the breakfast room and said to him, "Go on up to the barsati. If you hold your breath you can get through. I can't take Sundari because she wouldn't go and I can't carry her up the steps."

"No, memsaahib," he said, "I stay with you." I may never

180

encounter greater gallantry than Ram Prashad's that day; his loyalty seemed all the more touching since he was really afraid of Sundari. He pointed to the porch roof. We could reach it through a breakfast-room window. I snapped the leashes on the Cat while Ram Prashad opened the window and climbed out.

Sundari had never been asked to jump out a window on purpose and, since her zoo escapade, she had hardly wanted to. Anyway, no sensible leopard would do something she didn't think of first. But we had no time to let her debate, so I grabbed her up and threw her out the window. She was so surprised by such an unorthodox gesture that she had no time to protest. Had I not been so shaken I could never have heaved sixty-odd pounds of opinionated cat.

Ram Prashad snatched the leashes and hung on, quaking, while I hoisted myself out the window. Even under these circumstances, I realized how deep his devotion to Sundari was. For the last several months he had made sure there was a distance between them, and Sundari had done everything in her power to further his desire to worship from afar.

As I righted myself and took the leashes from Ram Prashad's trembling fingers, the telephone jangled. I wondered who would be calling in the midst of our fire, so I clambered back into the house to answer the fool thing. Sundari didn't like the roof in the first place; thinking that where I went, she should be, she came along, too. Ram Prashad, true to his word, followed suit. The call came from a nice man in AID wanting to know, "Mrs. Davis, have you called the fire department?"

The three of us groped our way back to the window, and in the same sequence as before, out we went again.

We could now hear the fire sirens. The AID office or Norma must have gotten through to them. A crowd, attracted by the smoke, was collecting on the roof of the garage next door. People jostled each other, laughed toothily, jockeyed for position, and pointed brown fingers our way. At the front of the house the murmur of a few had increased to the roar of a mob and we could see more people pouring down the alley to join the excitement.

The Rissler girls, Mary and Nancy, appeared with a step-ladder and set it up under the porch roof. "Here," they said, "You can crawl down." But by that time Sundari wouldn't jump down to the top of the ladder. So we sat. I looked at the laden roof on the other side of the fence and hoped it wasn't strong enough. Sundari and Ram Prashad trembled. I looked at the crowd of inanely curious and swore under my breath. They were actually savoring our helplessness.

After an aeon under the unwavering leers of strangers, we were reprieved by a fireman. He poked his head out the window and said, "Fire is gone—*sab jāaiyāa.*"

Bilious gray smoke still rolled through the hall and break-fast room, but the fireman could only have entered by way of the steps. So in we climbed again, thankful to escape prying eyes and ill-conceived humor.

Kristy's bathroom was relatively free of smoke and re-moved from the traffic of humanity. Sundari entered it as en-thusiastically as she usually left. Going back through the hall to the stairwell I shouldered through hordes of people. Fire-men, I supposed. I was soaked to the skin as I sloshed to the front door. There pandemonium reigned.

The hose brigade was spasmodically sousing everything that moved, even their fellow fire fighters. The force of water varied with the zest of the four men who manned the pump truck—they seemed to remember the fire in spurts. The leaky hose didn't, in fact, reach over the hedge and into our doorway. Bucket crews were chucking great blobs of wet sand willy-nilly into the hall, none of it landing near the fuse box. Hatchet men, wielding rusty claymores, were attacking the screen door as though to kill it. How the fire had been extinguished is a moot question.

Despite a dousing every two minutes, a peanut vendor had set up shop by our front door. His business was booming as he served the inquisitive sightseers. They, in turn, were being ushered into our house by obliging constables. The hub-bub brought the biirdii-wallah from down the street, and an enterprising ice cream salesman had wheeled his portable ice-box into our compound.

Our resident Nizam-ud-Din beggar assumed a humble, stoop-shouldered stance opposite the biirdii-wallah; his silver begging bowl and gold-rimmed spectacles certified his proficiency in the trade. The cycle-tire repairman and the chappal repairman, undeterred by automotive hazards, set up operations in the middle of the street.

At this point, Bob elbowed his way through the multitude. With him were Floyd Williams and two drivers and the office manager. Bob alleviated my anxiety by his comforting rhetoric:

"I don't know why you can't handle these picky little affairs yourself. Why must you always involve me in your productions?"

At that moment I was busy directing vehicular traffic—this time the dilapidated city ambulance. Its rear doors were actually tied together with a bit of twine. Since we didn't need ambulance services, it seemed only fair to send it to the back alley to succor those who fell off the garage roof.

Before I could turn my full attention on my solicitous spouse, Floyd came to the rescue: "Rocky, I don't think even you could create such a swinging scene on the spur of the moment."

The Risslers then intervened with invitations to all adults. "Join us for medicinal morning martinis!" they said. So we adjourned to their front porch for a ringside seat at the carnival. The only things missing were cotton candy and balloons.

The fire had been confined to the hallway. The door leading into the ground floor apartment was burnt, the fuse boxes and meters would all have to be replaced, and paint was charred to the second landing. Oily smoke-grime slathered the entire stairwell and two rooms in our apartment. But by far the biggest mess came from the fire fighters with their slaphappy hose and profligate sand buckets.

The downstairs door couldn't be closed—ostensibly to allow free entry to firemen and power-line repairmen. The real reason was the new bed of soggy river sand deposited during the deluge. It clogged everything except our riptide of excursionists. They disgorged into the house as though riding the spout of a fire hydrant. Under normal conditions, Indians strictly observe domestic privacy, but when their curiosity is aroused they know no limitations. Meddlesome inquisitiveness buoyed spectators in the gate, through the door, past the fire site, up the steps, and into our living quarters. After throwing out two unknown men who were wandering through the apartment, we stationed the servants to guard the hall and the top of the steps. They warded off further intrusions.

The Cat, of course, declined to root out invaders. She even forsook her favorite spot in the barsati hall. Instead, she retired to our bed and knotted her tail around herself for good measure. She wouldn't even hop to the top of the almirah because her avian vista was obstructed by linemen on the telephone pole.

This was the fifteen-month-old "mortal danger" we'd been living with. If anything she was more sensitive and more finely attuned to her family than ever, gentle with cats and kids and whimsically humorous with the servants. When she swaggered into the kitchen to sit grinning at Hari, he knew what she wanted, but always asked, just to hear her answer, "*Kyaa mantii*, Sundari? *Kyaa mantii*—what need?"

She told him the same thing every time with sparkling eyes and a head-wagging whine. Then Hari would produce the bone he had waiting for her in the refrigerator. When she took it from his hand, he would turn to me and say, "Memsaahib, she really understand!"

Murli, more than anyone else, suffered from Sundari's bumptiousness. He always seemed to be in the way when she galloped through the apartment, but he picked himself up smiling, "*Sundari acchii billii hai*—Sundari is good cat."

I had no argument on that score with either of them. She couldn't help being so big, and she *did* understand. And the bigger she got the more understanding she showed. The boys were gone but their letters began, "How's Sundari? Is she okay?" All of us would have staked our lives on the certainty that Sundari loved us as no other animal could have done. Even Bob had quit reminding me that "That Cat is YOUR animal."

Bob went so far as to tell callers that "she's more like a big dog than a cat"—a judgment I failed to share. She was

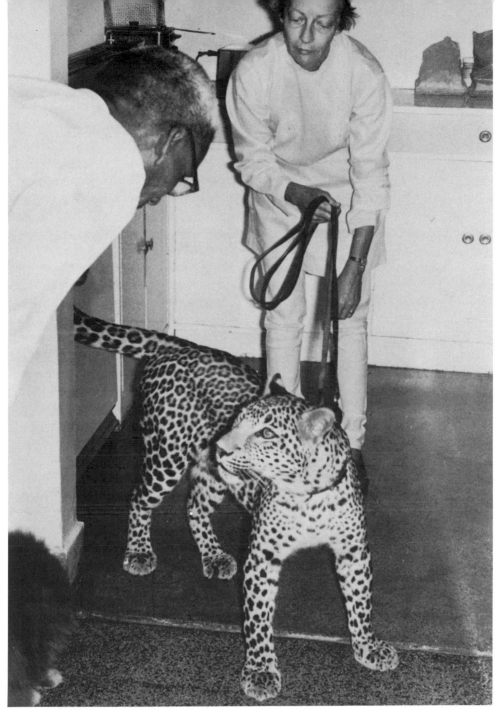

Baby Cat knew there was a handout in the offing when Hari asked, "Kyaa mantii, Sundari?" Rocky is holding the leash of eighteen-month-old Sundari. Charlotte Bush

not like a dog in any way: she was cat through and through. Much as she depended on us, she was perfectly capable of forming her own attitudes. Her reactions were strictly feline. When she misbehaved, it wasn't through ignorance but because she chose to ignore house rules. She never abjectly craved pardon, but she subscribed to discreet largesse and thus diverted attention from her worst transgressions. As far as I know, she was never sorry for her misdemeanors, just regretted being called on the carpet. She knew how to get around me in almost every case. All it took was a grin and I would find myself with arms wrapped around her and my nose buried in her neck saying, "Okay, Sundari, you win."

I was once asked by a reporter if I had ever punished her. And I couldn't think of a single instance when she had needed it. If Sundari was people-oriented, we were certainly leopard-oriented. This animal, poetry in motion, dominated our lives—not just Bob's and mine, but the children's as well. Her exquisite beauty lay far less in her luxurious pelt than in her gentleness, her great heart, and her uninhibited exuberance.

The nightly walks with Sundari and Kristy provided an atmosphere in which I learned to appreciate my older daughter in a special way. When we first came to India, she had been little more than a child, but in two years Kris had matured into a young adult. She handled Sundari as well as I, and sometimes took her out alone. But most times we sauntered through the neighborhood together talking of anything that came into our heads. Kris confided the happenings at school and I related Sundari's daily exploits. We were a closed corporation and preferred it so.

One night, just down the street from our house, we noticed tiny spotted owlets swirling around a street light after their dinner of insects. They are fascinating little creatures with huge eyes in swiveling heads, and we sat down in the street to watch them. We were so engrossed in the owls that we didn't see or hear the police patrol until they asked what we were doing. We pointed to the little birds.

They nodded their heads and backed away. They had accepted our late night perambulations with a leopard. Prob-

186

ably they felt that sitting on the damp pavement in the middle of a monsoon night was only another manifestation of Western eccentricity. For an hour we watched them swooping. Whenever they captured a particularly tasty morsel, they uttered little shrieks. Sundari was as enthralled as Kristy and I, and she "ulped" at especially graceful dives.

Fifty yards down the street there stretched a large maidan we seldom frequented because it was so poorly lighted, but when our interest in the owls paled, we meandered that way. Lack of illumination didn't hamper the Cat but it considerably dampened our own enthusiasm for that park. That night, though, she took us there, straining against the leashes with all her might. Neither Kris nor I could see anything special about it. There was no reason to deny her.

We were stepping cautiously to avoid breaking our legs in potholes, and Sundari moved just as deliberately. She took two or three steps and dropped to the ground as immobile as a statue. Suddenly we saw that she was stalking Nizam-ud-Din's holy herd. Patting our huntress, we fell into line, but our neophyte didn't know that pursuit should be silent.

Sundari's whiskers were standing rigidly at forty-five degrees from her nose. The tip of her tail flicked nervously. She was hot on the trail of a quarry. Concentration creased her brow, but her eyes sparkled with mischief. Finally, after a series of zig-zagging jerky dashes and flops to the ground we came to the first broad bovine backside. But the leopard, her prey within her grasp, didn't know what to do. She plunked her rear to the grass without the slightest idea of her next move. The unperturbed herd went on munching succulent greenery while Sundari pondered.

It was my deep-seated conviction that we had gone close enough to a cow, and had best make a strategic retreat in the face of overwhelming odds. But Sundari hadn't spent an hour executing guerrilla tactics for nothing. She shoved her nose into the beast for a good whiff of her adversary. And hurriedly withdrew with a grimace! Then she deliberately raised her forepaw and tapped the animal's rump ever so gently. The cow stepped away, still cropping her dinner, but the movement aroused the Cat's sporting instincts. She followed up with a swinging flat-pawed roundhouse. Startled, the bovine lumbered five paces and resumed her business.

Holy-cow-baiting was an exhilarating exercise. But Sundari miscalculated on her next move. One cow watched us, then lowered her head and MOOED. As smoothly as a team of trained gymnasts we jumped in unison and came down with legs pumping. However, the danger of enraged cattle only added to the sport, and there were other victims lurking in the shadows.

Sundari was almost upon the third rear when I realized from the huge shoulder hump that we were approaching the bull. It was unlikely that he would join our games as gently as his ladies. Kris noticed his bulk at almost the same moment, and both of us jerked on the leashes to haul Sundari away. But the Cat was unaware of cattle sexes and wasn't about to call off her game. She dug splayed paws into the ground, determined not to budge.

The bull heard our commotion and turned to see what it was about. We were perhaps fifty feet away when he decided to investigate. My terror was so complete that it didn't occur to me to drop the leashes and run for dear life. The leopard could have looked out for herself and escaped into a tree. But panting and begging Sundari to "Come on" we raced down the street, heaved ourselves through the gate, and slammed home the bar. The bull moved in no particular hurry; he just wanted to know what the furor was all about. But he was close enough to our heels to leave me hysterically jittery.

Safe, gasping with relief, we collapsed on the pavement. Just then two constables swung round the corner. It was more than we could stand with straight faces. We wrapped around the leopard and roared. Who but Kris and I could ever rejoice in the knowledge that a woman and a girl and a leopard had been chased down a midnight street by a holy cow?

188

12

THE LOVELIEST season in northern India is late September through mid-November. Another searing summer is over. Monsoon tempests have laid the dust devils for yet awhile, and all Delhi glows as though newly laundered. Wildly psychedelic gardens blaze with zinnias and nasturtiums, marigolds and cosmos. Trees reach revitalized jade limbs toward a cobalt canopy more intensely blue than anywhere else in the world. Stolid concrete houses, torpid in the rain, glimmer in fresh coats of hot pink, baby blue, or lemon yellow distemper. Maidans beckon lushly to hungry cattle, and the whole Gangetic Plain seems to sigh, giving itself up to the relief of gloriously clear days and cool nights.

Sundari was fifteen months old, almost sixteen. For three months she had been experimenting with her "saw." This sound is peculiar to leopards. With single-minded application, she had progressed through snuffling grunts and asthmatic

189

wheezes to a vibrant, full-throated timbre. In August she had sounded like a braying donkey with bronchitis. By October she could produce round, resonant, palpitating rumbles that came from her toes.

Neither a hunting call nor a mating invitation—she would not be reproductively mature until thirty months—her saw seemed to say, "Here I am! I walk alone and who will dare dispute my passage?"

And none does. The lordly tiger and immense elephant move aside. Chittal and warthog and jungle fowl take cover. So does man. He cowers in his acrylic-fiber camping nest against the onslaught of this jungle proclamation. But in our house, we reveled in Sundari's first sign of real maturity.

She perfected her saw whenever confined to quarters, day or night. We couldn't shut her up. The racket reverberated through the flat, bouncing off walls and echoing down the stairwell. Neighbors thought we were shredding Douglas firs with buzz saws. Apparently we had no big-game hunters in the vicinity, else we should have had complaints. No one connected the spine-shriveling rales with Sundari.

She had not merely fulfilled her ancestral pledge of splendor, she had far surpasssed it. Our early chagrin at her unkempt cubbish pelt had long since changed to awe. She moved with the lazy grace of an indolent ocean wave. Already longer and taller than an average mature male, she had heavy bones and her sinuous muscles recalled the tone of a fine race horse. She had the chest of an athlete, the brow of a philosopher. Fur, softer than eiderdown, glistened with good health.

It should have. She was downing five pounds of buffalo meat daily, not to mention the canned imported chicken, junior lamb, and ham that we added for variety. Nor the three indigenous egg yolks every morning. Hari and I had a silent conspiracy to conceal from our paymaster general exactly what Sundari's nutrition was costing him. Bob harped enough on the subject of replacing the household furniture. Besides, he often admonished me against involving him in my petty productions.

I had enough trouble concealing heated arguments from

his direct notice. Sundari could put up a strong defense when she felt her prerogatives infringed upon. As in the case of manicures. She preferred long pointed nails to the blunt ones I required; she had had a mighty aversion to having them clipped ever since one claw had been pulled out. While the boys were home, they pinned her to the floor while I operated, but after they left I had to wait until the Cat and her bedfellow were asleep to sneak up on her. Sometimes I could shear two before she woke up, but never more. And when she did awake, she reclaimed the paw with a jerk, slamming it back at me with a force designed to knock me senseless.

It was rare that I could trim eighteen claws at one sitting, yet she was forced to endure the procedure every ten days. It didn't concern her that Nuyan and Baby Cat suffered the same trial. Her own tenpenny nails could rip furniture to shreds in one swipe, and my family was not to be exposed to the same danger. Without conscious volition the claws of a great cat are deadly—far more lethal than fangs. Sundari had never extended hers in anger, but they grew apace with the rest of her and the power to amputate lay within each paw.

For all her intensity in a disagreement, her thumping belts were not delivered in bad humor. Nor viciously. They were protestations of a thwarted child, spirited but not malicious. Her bites were in the same vein. She had no intention of inflicting damage, else she would have done so. She simply gave fair warning that we were treading on leopard dignity. Sometimes her flashing fangs clamped around an arm painfully enough to bring tears, so that we got the message. But when she released her grip and massaged the spot with her Brillo tongue, there would be no mark at all to show for it. Not even a tiny blood blister.

Bob escaped such feline reprimands. He fooled with her less, of course. But she judged it would be extremely unwise to tangle with him. Then, too, he only laughed with her, never at her. He was consistently steady toward Sundari, lending his support when she desperately needed it. She seemed aware that when the chips were down he was her bulwark, beyond reproach.

191

She sometimes grew indignant. She liked nothing better than to spread herself out on the stereo cabinet to snooze in the afternoon sun, but she never quite understood that a three-foot surface couldn't accommodate seven feet four inches of dappled animation. Luxuriating in the autumn sunshine, she would groan pleasurably and stretch her legs; inevitably she toppled to the floor. And we laughed. Scraping together the shards of her dignity she would glare at us accusingly as though we had planned her downfall. In high dudgeon she would sway to the kitchen for Hari's sympathy.

She never minded about dignity, though, when we called, "Sundari? Want to go for a ride?" Her great tail thumped the walls and banister as she loped down the steps in two easy strides between landings.

One October evening when I called her she got more than she bargained for. All through the summer we had been getting emergency calls from teen-agers in charge of the student union asking us to fill vacancies created by chaperones who didn't show up. Bob and I took our regular turns at the chaperone chore, but we felt that too often the kids were being left in the lurch by parents more concerned with their own pleasures than with their children. More and more often, Bob and I were called to substitute, and Sundari was spending more weekend evenings in confinement.

That Saturday night, Bob had just returned from a field trip haggard and dusty. All he wanted was a bath and bed, but the telephone jangled an SOS. "Give me half an hour," I told the youngster—and then turned to Sundari: "Okay, big girl! Now you're going to be a chaperone."

I had my reasons. Some of the same parents too busy to help with a teen-age evening were inconsistent in other ways. They would send their children to our house to play with Sundari, but if they saw the same youngsters near the Cat in our car, they would raise a fuss. Maybe the word should get around: when parents can't chaperone, a leopard makes a grand substitute.

Ping-pong balls were flying and the juke box exhaled rasping rock wails. Ash trays overflowed, paper napkins littered

Spread out on the stereo cabinet at sixteen months. Davis

the floor, and spilled 7-Up bubbled off tables. Everything looked perfectly normal to the Cat. She'd spent half her life in rooms that looked and sounded the same way.

Crowds didn't mean anything; as long as they smelled like Right Guard and Head and Shoulders, Sundari thought they were her kids. She spied the chest-high counter that separated the two rooms. Long enough to support her frame, the counter allowed her to survey the premises and also provided a throne for receiving the multitudes. She even had one or two favorites to sit beside her.

The evening was a huge success. Sundari played the gracious hostess. And those young adults, so far from the restraints of American suburbs, idolized her. They patted and petted and talked to their exotic guardian. She glowed with goodwill. The noisy activity revolved around her, and she understood. She'd been in the middle of teen-age turmoil all her life.

Without being told, the youngsters knew not to press her. They had the thoughtful knack of waiting until Sundari herself gave them the signal that they could touch her. And they enjoyed her. There is just something electric about physical contact with a great cat; one feels elevated to the level of the elect. Initiates can whisper to themselves, "This hand knows the downy silk of a leopard neck, and this leg has felt the coarse kiss of a leopard's tongue."

After Sundari's impeccable evening as a chaperone, not one parent protested. But our hint bore results. Thereafter, the student union had no trouble finding parents to do their duty.

With Sundari as our bodyguard, we had always felt secure. But then we began to wonder. It was Bob's colleague, K. B. Singh, who started us thinking. K. B. was the only Indian national other than our servants whom Sundari accepted as a true friend. Whenever he came to Delhi from Ludhiana in the Punjab, he stayed with us. His relations with the Cat were always pleasant. He freely told her that while she was beautiful, he was wary of her kittenish actions. Not once did he ever say or imply that we were not safe with this great cat. Sundari sensed that he accepted her as an individual. But the rest of us weren't aware of how close his attitude was to our own until he warned me.

"I don't think you should be taking Sundari out so late," he said. "The streets are full of thieves and aren't safe for you."

I was surprised at his concern. I could think of no one safer than we. But K. B. had considered Sundari one of us, not a leopard to be feared but a human to be afraid. It hadn't occurred to him that she insulated us from attack.

His advice made us wonder, though, at what distance a stranger could identify Sundari as a leopard. Under a street lamp, of course, there was no question. But when her coat blended with the shadows—as she preferred—we could not discern her outline at twenty feet. At fifteen feet, we could distinguish a dim outline; we might also note a flicking patch of white ear or gleaming chest. But to recognize Sundari as a feline, not a large dog, a person would have to see her from ten feet. Even then, the awful realization might take several seconds. Precious little time if she felt endangered.

There was no question in my mind that Sundari would never attack anyone unprovoked. She wasn't above scaring people, and she had some paralyzing ways of doing it. One evening when she and I were walking alone, we sat down on a stone bench in our favorite maidan. She stretched out with her head on my lap while I smoked a cigarette and gave her a lesson in astronomy. Not that I knew much about the subject; I just liked to talk to her, and I could identify Orion. Across the park another lounger's cigarette winked. For some reason I felt he was observing us closely. He couldn't see the Cat, and I knew he was going to speak to me. Perhaps he simply wanted to know why I was out so late at night. If he was just being neighborly I didn't want Sundari to unnerve him, so I laid my hand on her head and sat still.

He paused on the sidewalk behind us, still unaware of Sundari, quietly poised, then took a step toward the bench. She kept waiting. Then he leaned over the back of the bench to ask, "Will you give me a light . . .?"

With a guttural warning, Sundari stood up. Her forepaw placed on the back of the bench, she towered over the stranger.

He stood mesmerized, shuddering. He seemed unable to move. She made no attempt to follow up her threat: it was enough that she was what she was.

I tugged gently at the leashes to make her sit down again. I then turned to him. "I think you should go on," I said. "The *thendua* doesn't like strangers to speak to me."

He took me at my word, slowly at first and then faster. And faster. Until he was running as fast as he could. It served him right. Why should he want a light when he had just put out a cigarette?

Shortly after that, however, we were strolling with Harley Watts, another of our PCVs, when we met three men. By their clothing we could tell they were of the serving sweeper class. We passed under a street light so they knew without doubt that the animal with us was not a dog. They turned and followed us, making unpleasant vulgar remarks in Hindi, and then tried to get Sundari's attention with some idiot mewling noises. I should have ignored them, but I didn't. Swinging Sundari around to face them, I called, "*Sundari! Khanna vāahāa*—dinner there!"

They dropped quickly from sight, and we thought they had gone their own way. But two blocks farther, a brick sped past Sundari's nose. It struck sparks as it hit the pavement. In a second the air was full of flying stones. All aimed at us.

We were three blocks from home and outnumbered. Sundari and I took cover behind a scraggly hedge while Harley gave chase. We knew that anyone who mounted so cowardly an attack wouldn't stay nearby when confronted.

Just then a cab pulled up beside our refuge and a Western woman stepped out. Almost shouting, I asked, "Please? Will you send the cabbie back to Nizam-ud-Din Police Station? Tell them Sundari is being stoned. They'll know who she is!"

A voice from inside the cab called, "*I* know who she is! Chelloo!"

The lady, European by her accent, said she would stay with us until her husband returned. She crouched beside me cooing to Sundari as though all eighty pounds of enormous cat were a babe in arms. Between comforting words for Sundari she said to me, "I remember when I first came to Delhi. You lent me your phone one day."

One meets the nicest people squatting under jasmine bushes.

Harley and the cab reappeared at the same time. "Those hooligans are gone," said Harley.

"And the police are on their way," reported the man in the cab. But knowing that Delhi police are occasionally dilatory, we didn't expect them to materialize before dawn. We decided to make for home by a roundabout way.

We ambled along without incident until three nicely dressed men on two scooters passed us. Their scooters halted and they backed up. Two of the men lived in Nizam-ud-Din, and knew about Sundari. Their questions were intelligent, and I enjoyed telling them about the leopard. Sundari, thoughtful after the last encounter, sat down patiently to wait for us to finish the conversation.

While we chatted, two bicycle policemen pulled up to us. "You are under arrest!" they told our new friends.

"No, no!" we shouted. "There's been a mistake." Harley and I assured the constables that these were not the troublemakers, only innocent bystanders.

In broken English one said, "No. I am here to defend you."

It took half an hour's wrangling in pidgin Hinglish to convince the rescuers that we were safe.

Though the evening ended in laughter, we still recalled the bricks and stones. Had I not been so sure of my neighborhood, the incident might never have happened. Lack of response to our tormentors might have cooled their interest. On the other side of the coin, we met neighbors who had proved that Nizam-ud-Din East had taken Sundari to its heart.

It had actually been done: a great cat lived in harmony with humankind because people felt part of her existence. People we didn't know knew us and our leopard. They weren't afraid of her but were interested in her welfare and willing to rise to her defense. They didn't see her as a predator, but as a pet to be protected. We shared her gratefully, because they all had a sense of responsibility to her.

If for no other reason, alien residents long remember Delhi for its brotherhood of taxi-driving confidence men. Children are especially at the mercy of their venality; drivers often take them miles out of their way while a meter with filed teeth clicks off an impossible fare. No two meters read alike, but the average fare between our house and the school was between 4.30 rupees and 4.60 rupees. Within those bounds, we paid without complaint, but when more was demanded we paid 4.50 rupees—and let the pirate count himself lucky that we didn't record his license number.

One fall afternoon Sundari and I were sunning on the barsati when Jan burst into the house yelling, "Mom? Mom, come down here and make this taxi-wallah leave us alone."

Jan and two friends had ridden home in a cab with a crooked meter. They had come straight from school, but the meter read 6.70 rupees. The girls had given the driver a five-rupee note. They knew he had been well paid, but this thief wasn't to be put off. He followed them to the door. Usually, it was easy to change their minds when they tried to cheat the children. I could walk onto the front porch and call down, "Take his license number. We'll report him!"

Invariably the threat of a meter check made the crooks retreat. This time it didn't work. Jan had had the presence of mind to bolt the screen door, but this robber-baron wasn't to be deterred. He must have thought, too, that the girls were coming into an empty house. He pressed the bell insistently, pushed his nose into the screen.

Leaning over the balustrade I could see him leering at the girls. I called to him, "Are you sure you want R 6.70?"

But his attention was riveted on the three blond girls. He merely nodded. I asked him again, just to make sure. As Sundari and I rounded the first landing he was ogling the children in a disquieting fashion. He didn't see Sundari—not until she reared to press her pink nose against his.

His nostrils flared, his mouth drooped, he squeezed his

eyes shut. He peeked—and snapped his eyes shut again. Nothing separated him from this beast but a flimsy screen.

He began backing away from the door, hands cupping his face. Sundari stepped out the door, and the poor fellow's head began to wobble on its axis. As we backed away he placed each foot with utmost care. Sundari cocked her head. She'd never seen anyone act like that before, and took a step toward him. His nerves snapped completely. Keening an anguished yelp he flung himself through the gate toward his cab.

We could laugh off such incidents, but another problem loomed large. Home leave was approaching. United States government employees go to India for two-year tours. We had extended ours for one extra year. But three years is the limit without a visit to the United States. The government has good reason for this rule. Overseas personnel can get out of touch with their own country and foreign frustrations can weigh heavy in three years.

We had enjoyed Sundari for nearly a year and a half. In six months we would have to go home. For a multitude of reasons Sundari could not go with us. Even if Indian export regulations could have been waived for us, we would have no settled location in the United States; we would be depending upon the generosity of friends and relatives to put us up. Hosts, no matter how sympathetic, would have neighbors likely to protest. In addition, the cost of her transportation and food would be enormous—especially for a family paying university tuitions.

So our decision about Sundari's future was upon us. Squirm as I would, there was no escape. I lay awake nights wondering how to avoid the problem. I had sworn I would put Sundari to sleep rather than return her to the zoo. I knew in my heart I couldn't do what I had said. I couldn't kill my leopard without first trying every other possibility.

Bob, understanding and almost as torn as I, bore with my tears and protestations. How did I know the animal wouldn't turn out to be vicious? How was I supposed to know she'd turn out to be a person?

"I couldn't tell I'd love a leopard so much," I would sob.

And Bob would reply, "Well, you should have. We brought two cats ten thousand miles for that very reason, didn't we?"

But Nuyan and Baby Cat were different. If they had been handed to someone else, they could have adjusted.

Dick Matsuura told the game warden at Corbett National Park about our plight. "With training," said the warden, "perhaps Mrs. Davis could return the leopard to the wild state."

But in India it wouldn't have worked. She had never been away from us and hardly ever away from our home. Game preserves in India are multipurpose areas; they are cut over for timber and grazed by herds of cattle and goats. Sundari would be in constant danger from herdsmen with guns; she would certainly seek the only society she knew—human.

Finally, Bob made me face up to the only solution. "You could stay in India while I take the kids home," he offered. But I couldn't do that. I wasn't ready to cut my ties.

"Okay," said Bob, "if you won't stay here and you can't kill her, there's only one alternative. Put her into the zoo." He knew I'd been avoiding that idea, pretending it didn't exist. "If you credit Sundari with so much intelligence, what makes you think she can't or won't adjust?"

When it came to that, I knew she had mind enough; the question was heart. She had done every other thing we had asked of her. But the truth was that I didn't think I could stand to see my beloved Cat behind bars.

Yet we had to try. If she couldn't make the adjustment, we would have to destroy her. It would take months of work, months of watching her fight against things she couldn't understand. If she succeeded it meant heartbreak.

I picked up the phone. Murli and Hari were weeping silently in the kitchen. Bob had disappeared, and the girls were hiding in Kristy's bedroom. The house was silent as a tomb. Mr. Sankhala answered the ring.

"Hello," I said, "This is Rocky Davis. I've made a decision." My willpower broke, loosing a flood of sobs.

200

13

THAT FIRST Saturday morning, Bob asked, "Do you want me to come along?"

"No," I said, "I don't think so. We'll have to do it alone after this. Besides, I want Sundari sitting on the front seat when we drive into that zoo." Everyone would see how reliable and proud she was.

"You're not going to back out at the last minute?" he asked.

"There just isn't any other way," I said.

So we returned to the Delhi Zoo to begin Sundari's re-training program. She would spend each day there without me, but would come home at six each evening. Until she grew accustomed to the new routine, Sundari would take her meals at home.

We would be reversing all her early conditioning. She would be forced into self-reliance. Heretofore, we had taught her always to rely upon our judgment and protection. Now she would have to face the vagaries of people whose interest was not her beauty but how violently they could make her react to their presence. There was no guarantee of success. But the alternative for Sundari—that vital, whimsical, beautiful, loving animal—was death.

Induction day was harder than I had imagined possible. We found a large group of Delhi newspapermen waiting for us at Mr. Sankhala's office. Neither Sundari nor I felt up to the encounter. So, while Mr. Sankhala talked with the press, he assigned an assistant director, Mr. L., to take us to Sundari's caged quarters.

"You will be dealing with Mr. L. on a daily basis for this project," Mr. Sankhala explained.

The choice was unfortunate. Apparently Sundari recalled the round, pock-marked Mr. L. from her traumatic beating and confinement here. Instantly she warned him with a snarl.

Wisely, Mr. L. chose to ride in a jeep rather than sit beside Sundari. I could have put her in the back of our car, of course, but I wanted all the zoo personnel to see what complete confidence I had in her.

To my horror, Mr. L. led us to the same three-by-five-foot cellblock where she had been confined before. For both of us, the painful memory rushed back. Clearly, Sundari had no desire to repeat the experience.

Herculean effort is always required to dislodge a reluctant leopard from a car. This time Sundari hooked her claws on the knobs and wound her tail on other projections. For some minutes I was too busy to realize the Cat was actually enjoying the tussle. She grinned at me. She had found an audience with Mr. L. and the gaping bevy of keepers. They took in the scene and understood nothing. But I had to get her out soon because I didn't have the strength for a protracted engagement. Then our pretense about who controlled whom would be exposed.

"Please step back where she can't see you," I asked. But the keepers only grinned foolishly and stood pat.

Finally a frantic jerk on the leash brought the Cat out of the car and she allowed herself to be pulled into her cell.

The bars were slammed home and I fled. Her "come back" barks followed me to the gates. The sound of her pleas clearly said, "Judas, don't leave me here!"

Saturday mornings at our house were usually a time for leisure, sunbaths on the barsati, and gardening among the bougainvillaea. But that morning the sun vanished behind a cloud burkha. Jan and Kris kept to their rooms. Hari, who should have been at the market, stayed in our room whispering nasally to Murli. The bearer himself used the corner of our top sheet to wipe his tears. Murli was sobbing audibly.

"How did it go?" Bob asked me. I began to cry. My morale improved not at all during the day. By four that afternoon, Bob said, "Go get your Cat. It's enough for one day. Tell them that *I* said she's to come home now."

Indian males understand that women must do as their menfolk order. I routed Mr. L. from his office and told him Dr. Davis said we could not wait until six o'clock. Mr. L. inserted the key into our lock without a shadow of emotion. Sundari cowered in a far corner of the cage until the leashes were secured to the harness. Then she leaped for the car. Not until she sat securely in the front seat did she turn toward Mr. L. Sitting bolt upright, she emitted a Vesuvian blast rumbling up from her innards, gathering force as it erupted from her throat. Knowing her as I did, I still found it difficult to associate Sundari with the incredible sound she had mustered. The sheer volume was stupefying. It engulfed the car with deafening intensity like the core of an earthquake. Any doubt Mr. L. might have had about her unreliability was rent asunder. As the roar echoed over the zoo, Mr. L. was shaken. His face showed pure hatred.

In previous encounters with this man, I had formed the impression that he lost no love on large cats. He even seemed to distrust those who did. Now Sundari had dashed his poise. His pocked face darkened.

"If that cat were left to me," he glowered, "I should beat her into submission in a week."

But during the next weeks, he would discover that it wasn't quite that simple. "Your life is at stake," he insisted.

"Once and for all you and that animal should be separated."

After her monumental roar that day, it seemed as though Sundari had exhausted her energy. She slouched on the seat until we cleared the zoo gates. Then each revolution of the wheels seemed to give her more confidence. By the time we reached our front door, she had recovered her old aplomb. She bounded past Hari and Murli, standing by to greet her, and gave each a madcap whack with her tail. She took the steps five at a time. Kris and Jan collided with her in the hall and received exuberant kisses. Bob sighed as we plunged through the barsati door; he would be safe from the sound of sobs and hysterics until Monday morning.

This would be the pattern of our lives for the next months. When Sundari was in the house, all of us relaxed, happy to have a few more hours with her. When she was gone, we waited tensely for her to come back. No one asked me how she did in the zoo because such questions invariably brought a flood of tears. Bob sympathetically bore with my sobbing and ranting. Murli grimly endured my bad temper, and Hari put fewer chilis into the curry.

During the first ten days I could see no progress at all. Sundari grew leary of getting into the station wagon. Indeed, she only went to the front door with coaxing, for all too often it led to her private purgatory. In the cage she huddled in a dejected heap. She averted her eyes from the front; if she didn't see her surroundings perhaps things would change. At home she was preoccupied with consideration for others—a novelty. Not even Bob would have complained if she had gone on a rampage. We actually expected her to do just that. Instead, she was so pathetically eager to please us that we found it hard to remember how difficult it had once been to restrain her. She seemed to be trying to prove how little inconvenience it was to have her around. She even allowed Baby Cat and Nuyan to escape from her ministrations at their first yawp of annoyance. Appreciative as we were of the peace, we missed her old bounce.

At night she stretched full length between Bob and me and lay as still as a pillow. We each had our three inches and

Rocky had to coax nineteen-month-old Sundari to get her to the front door, but it looks the other way around. Charlotte Bush

Sundari, twenty months old, with Baby Cat and Rocky, pathetically eager to prove she is trustworthy and gentle. This was the last photograph taken of her at home. Davis

she her three feet of middle while she slept the sleep of exhaustion. There was no need to take her out for walks in the hours of darkness, yet I missed our shared solitude.

Morning and evening, our confrontations with Mr. L. increased the tension. Fearing Sundari and disliking me, Mr. L. insisted on standing beside us as I got the Cat in and out of the cage. It was useless to point out how much easier the job would have been without him. Perhaps he had been instructed to watch us, but whatever his reasons, he ogled us the whole time. Sundari soon identified him with the cause of her distress. She growled at him. And her roars soared over the whole zoo. Inside her cell, the sound reverberated off the walls and left my ears ringing.

After each scuffle, Mr. L. would smile, "Mrs. Davis, you don't know how terrifying it is to listen while you work! I'm never sure you are coming out alive." He smiled while he said it.

I suppressed all retorts. I could not afford to offend anyone in the zoo—for Sundari's sake. Her behavior did not help our cause. Particularly when she chose to leave Mr. L. and his troops shuddering with fear.

Mr. L. never lost sight of us or his purpose. The atavistic conduct he daily reported made the whole administrative staff apprehensive. What if I should be banned from the cages— as protection for myself? We could not deny that she did snort, snarl, groan, growl, roar, and resist. Without exaggeration, every time she tuned up her *basso profundo,* every cat in the zoo chorused her sentiment.

It was not true, however, that any of this protest was directed toward me. As proof I could offer myself. I wasn't dead, maimed, mauled, or even scratched. I outweighed the leopard by only ten pounds. Inch for inch, she had the advantage of me by approximately twenty-five. In the forty years between our births, I had been coddling ninety-five pounds, while from infancy she had followed a fitness program that could have been a model for Olympic athletes.

Mr. L. would have had a coronary had he guessed that Sundari's claws had not been clipped since the day we began our experiment. The incongruities in the situation irritated him enough. The longer I retained my health while Sundari refused to accept any part of zoo life, the less weight could be attached to his professional opinions.

At Mr. L.'s prompting, the zoo veterinarian remembered there were other animals in our home. Perhaps they harbored disease that could be transmitted to the zoo via Sundari. I presented him with vaccination certificates against rabies, distemper, hepatitis, and leptospirosis for all our cats, including Sundari. Since the zoo could not boast a single animal with similar protection, the vet backed down.

Our zoo routine brought my social life to a halt. To go out when Sundari was home meant leaving her in a bathroom. I couldn't do that when she had so few hours with us. And our time was running out. I saved errands to run when Sundari could go along so she wouldn't always associate a car ride with the zoo. Bob had taken Kris, Jan, and Hari to Goa for Christmas, leaving Murli to minister to my needs. We had promised the girls another holiday at the beach, but because I couldn't leave the Cat, they had gone without me.

The tiny isolation cell that the zoo had assigned us was so dismally depressing that I began lobbying for larger quarters. The leopard couldn't exercise in such cramped quarters. Her coat was losing its luster, and I thought if she had the chance to move around more, she might be more relaxed. She would not groom herself until she grew calmer. She did groom herself at home, but in the zoo she stayed too nervous to give hygiene a thought. Larger quarters brought disadvantages; she would be exposed to the bear-baiting mentality of zoo visitors. Still, sooner or later, she would have to face them. Better with my support than without, I reasoned. And human hecklers could not alter the final outcome.

The new housing was luxurious by zoo standards. The stone cellblock contained eight roomlets and two octagonal grass enclosures. Raja, a personable young jaguar, had one exercise area and three cubicles. Three of the remaining cubicles were allotted to Sundari. Deep piles of straw covered Sundari's rooms wall to wall—a concession to her old standard

208

Sundari, nineteen months old, and Rocky. So few hours left to-gether. Charlotte Bush

of living. Her commodious outdoor arena, roofed in mesh, included a forked neem tree for climbing.

Unfortunately, the switch from tenement to town house suited Sundari no better. She refused to move for her keeper, a minute, chocolaty Rajasthani. She realized that good behavior brought no time off. The keeper's attempts at gentle persuasion failed to move her out and into the sunshine. She snarled her defiance. Her only incentive to go outside came when she heard our car. Each day when I arrived, she was pacing along the bars, whining and barking, "Come here." On the few occasions that I walked to the zoo I found her cramped onto a tiny windowsill six feet above the floor. She aggressively defied anyone to move her. Yet her animosity wilted when she saw me.

She would not eat at the zoo. Regularly the keeper tossed her a generous serving of raw, antique goat meat. Day after day the revolting mess lay rotting in her cage.

Gradually we increased the periods of her confinement. She would spend one night and return the next evening. Still she would eat only at the apartment.

As the length of her incarcerations increased to three, four, and finally to five days at a time, I spent more and more time sitting with her in the shade of the neem tree. Regardless of the part I had played in indenturing her to this life, she had more confidence when I was with her. At first she would slouch against me, hissing softly to tell me she wanted to go home. Then she began retreating to the surly comfort of the cement roof over the doorway to her cell; there she was out of reach for the worst trash—the lit cigarette butts, broken pop bottles, and the firecrackers tossed by the visiting population. These tokens of public interest couldn't touch her, but the visitors' yammering, hooting, prancing, and face-making could hardly be ignored. She lay tense above them, snarling. It was hard to realize how human beings—elevated above all other animals by their ability to learn and reason—could sink so low.

But we had to go on.

I blatantly bribed the Rajasthani keeper with cigarettes

Sundari, at twenty-three months, has retreated to the surly comfort of the cement roof over the doorway to her cell in the zoo. This is the last picture we took. Davis

in the hope that he would refrain from reporting all he saw to Mr. L. But Sundari herself gave her enemy the weapon he wanted. To her he represented all her pain and frustration. One morning he leaned over the safety rail, ogling the leopard. Suddenly her body hurtled through the air to slam against the bars a foot above his head. Recoiling, she crouched, ready to spring again. She bellowed loud her hatred and defiance. I had to admit it: she wanted to kill him. If she had been able to reach him, she would have killed.

Sheer surprise and fear toppled Mr. L. The plump administrator sprawled then bounced like a basketball on his way to the office. His eloquently retreating back disappeared as Sundari slipped back to lick my hand. She seemed to say, "Well, this time we've given him something to think about."

She certainly had. Now Mr. L. had proof positive that she would kill. In all honesty, I could not deny the fact. Beyond that, I could not have prevented her from trying to kill Mr. L.—not even if I had anticipated her action. If she should make the same attempt outside the cage, then Mr. L. would be doomed. And I would be responsible.

For an hour we debated the situation in the director's office. Then we agreed on a compromise. "We can test her with live bait," said Mr. Sankhala. "If she kills the bait, then, Mrs. Davis, you will be barred from entering the cage. And you must not take her home again."

Sundari had neither the knowledge nor the inclination to kill for food. She certainly didn't relish raw meat, and she had lived in harmony a long time with little animals. I was confident of these things, but it would have to be proved to the director and his assistants. If she failed to kill, we would continue my way a little longer—but Mr. L. would be transferred to other duties. He learned of his dismissal with great relief, and so did I. Confident that the director would get his reports from Sundari's Rajasthani keeper, my local tobacco purchases soared.

The first trial was conducted with a tattered pigeon of indefinite grayish plumage. Initially, the bird flew against the bars, seeking a way out. But soon, he fluttered to rest on

Sundari's tail. The mighty leopard lay gazing fondly at company while it made cooing sounds at her. Next morning the pigeon remained in remarkably good health; it had obviously found a new friend. Once again, the Cat had proved herself.

As an adversary, the pigeon had been a flop. It was removed. Sundari's next cellmate was an infinitely inane chicken. White, scrawny, and ancient, it skittered and squawked stupidly. Sundari sat with head cocked and whiskers alert, smiling genially at the addled thing. Three days later, the chicken was placidly scratching for grubs, clucking companionably to the leopard. Sundari stood guard over it. I finally took the bird out and gave it to the keeper, who had no leopardlike reservations about killing a chicken.

Sundari simply could not kill. She had never been taught and there was no point in prolonging this unnecessary experiment. She would have to grow a lot hungrier before she would make an attempt to get her own meals.

In three months we had gradually increased the length of her stays in the zoo to five days, but still she refused to eat except at home. Her coat was tatty with accumulated dust and muss. At home she worked patiently to comb it smooth, but weekly baths didn't suffice to maintain its old beauty.

One day I passed the cage of Meenu, Sundari's mother. Meenu was the one zoo leopard that I trusted sufficiently to pet. She came to the side of her cage and rubbed against the bars. I reached my hand inside and, to her great pleasure, stroked her lustrous coat. She harbored no ill will, though we had taken her last and only cub. In a way, I had replaced Meenu as Sundari's mother. And now, as part of life's relentless rhythm of change, I too must give up Sundari.

"If the cub can manage with formula feeding," I had said long ago, "then we shouldn't take her back to see her mother. It would only confuse her."

We had been quite right. And thus, the tiny cub Sundari —that toylike kitten with a bandaged paw—had swiftly adapted to her new life. Weren't we now facing the same adjustment all over again?

"When Sundari shows me that she can eat in the zoo,"

I told Mr. Sankhala, "then I'll know that she can survive. We shouldn't confuse her. After that, I will leave her in the zoo."

And still she fasted. At home she wolfed down kilos of her meat and preened herself as always. But time was running out. If she could not eat in the zoo before time for us to leave India, then we had no recourse. We could not permit her to die from sadness and starvation.

"Murli," I said one Friday, "tonight you must not feed Sundari. I shall give her all that she can have—and you are not to feed her on the sly."

I measured out a small meal, and when she had ravenously gulped it down, she begged for more.

"No, Sundari," I said. I hugged her, and fought back tears. "I'll cook you a good meal, Pretty. But you must eat it at the zoo."

We cooked her a tempting dish of ground buffalo meat and added her favorite baby lamb. On Monday morning, in her cage at the zoo, she sniffed it, licked it tentatively—and then she ate. In sadness and in gratitude, I wept. Sundari, age twenty-two months, would live. I had won the battle and lost my Cat.

Glossary

AAP-KAA KHANNA VAAHÃA HAI. There's your dinner.
AID. Agency for International Development, under the United
    States Department of State.
ALMIRAH. Cabinet, wardrobe.
BAAGH. Pharsi for tiger.
BAARII. Large (feminine ending).
BAHUT KHARAB. Very bad.
BAKSHISH. Gratuity or bribe.
BARSATI. Flat roof sometimes used as a garden.
BEARER. Male servant who does light housework and serves
    meals. Sometimes the bearer doubles as a sweeper, in
    which case he also does heavy chores such as washing
    floors and cleaning bathrooms.
BHUUKII. Hungry.
BIIRDII. Indian cigarette.
BIIRDII-WALLAH. Cigarette vendor.
BILLII. Cat.

BURKHA. Muslim woman's shroudlike garment.

BUS. Stop or enough.

CHAPPAL. Thong sandal.

CHARPOY. Indian string cot.

CHEETAH. Spotted, hence cheetah-billii is spotted cat.

CHELLOO. Go fast, a demand for speed.

CHITTAL. Small spotted Asian antelope.

CHOWKIDAAR. Watchman or guard.

COOLIE. Unskilled laborer.

DHOBI. Laundryman.

DHOTI. One-piece garment worn wrapped around the hips and pulled between a man's legs to form a sort of trouser.

GODOWN. Storeroom.

GOSHT. Meat.

GOSHT-WALLAH. Meat man.

JUMNA RIVER. Part of Ganges watershed system, India's second holiest river (pronounced Yumna).

KITNAA BAARAA. How big.

KILO. 2.2 pounds, part of the metric system of weights.

KYAA MANTII. What is needed or necessary.

LEE JAAOO. Get out or go away.

MAIDAN. Park or open space.

MALI. Gardener.

MEMSAAHIB. Polite address to a lady (Pharsi word).

NULLAH. Dry creek bed or open drainage ditch.

PEON. Assistant, not a laborer.

PYE-DOG. Scavenger dog belonging to no one.

PIICHII JAAOO. Go back.

SAAHIB. Formal address to a gentleman (Pharsi word).

SAB JAAIYĒE. All gone.

SHIIKAAR. Hunt or hunter.

SADHU. Hindu holy man.

SUNDARI. The beautiful one, pronounced Soon̈-duh-reé.

THENDUA. Leopard, also a Pharsi word. To my knowledge, there is no Sanseritic derivation for leopard other than *cheetah-billi*.

THIIK HOOGAA. It will be all right.

VOO BAHUT ACCHII HAI. She is very good.

WALLAH. Noun additive changing it to an adjective, i.e., *banana-wallah* means banana peddler, literally the banana-one.

216